Interview Skills
that **Win** the **Job**

D0964155

Interview Skills that **Win** the **Job**

Simple techniques for answering all the tough questions

MICHAEL SPIROPOULOS

ALLEN&UNWIN

First published in 2005

Copyright © Michael Spiropoulos 2005

Allen & Unwin
83 Alexander Street
Crows Nest NSW 2065
Australia
Phone: (61 2) 8425 0100
Fax: (61 2) 9906 2218
Email: info@allenandunwin.com
Web: www.allenandunwin.com

National Library of Australia
Cataloguing-in-Publication entry:

Spiropoulos, Michael, 1959- .
   Interview skills that win the job: simple techniques for
   answering all the tough questions.

   ISBN 1 74114 188 5.

   1. Employment interviewing. I. Title.

658.31124

Set in 9.5/13 pt Stone Serif by Bookhouse, Sydney
Printed in Australia by McPherson's Printing Group

10 9 8 7 6 5 4 3 2 1

This book is dedicated to
Suzanne Smith
for her love and support

Contents

Introduction: The path to **interview** success

Interview Skills that Win the Job offers an innovative and exciting approach to developing interview skills. As well as letting you know what's needed to succeed at interviews, it goes one important step further and demonstrates how you can prepare your own answers including exercises designed to improve your skills. People who consistently succeed at interviews are those who take the time to prepare their own answers rather than simply using answers they have read or heard elsewhere.

Whether you're a recent school leaver or a seasoned professional, this book will show you how to prepare highly effective answers and how to deliver them in a confident manner whilst establishing that all-important rapport with interviewers.

The book recognises that one of the major obstacles to successful interviewing is organising a vast amount of detail about what you've done in previous jobs (or at school or university) and expressing this information in a clear and convincing way at the interview. The book has been designed specifically to prevent you from:

- giving those long-winded answers that drive interviewers to distraction;
- failing to mention important key achievements and kicking yourself afterwards;

- being stumped by certain questions and not providing an intelligent response;
- failing to build rapport and trust.

In addition to teaching you how to respond to popular interview questions and distinguishing a good answer from a bad one, *Interview Skills that Win the Job* will go through the specific steps you need to establish rapport and trust during the course of the interview. The reason for this is simple: if you fail to establish rapport and trust, it is highly unlikely that you will get the job—no matter how technically brilliant your answers are.

The skills and techniques you will develop from reading this book will remain with you for the rest of your working life. They will immeasurably improve your chances of winning those hard-to-get jobs and contribute to a rewarding career.

Interview Skills
that **Win** the **Job**

1 Interview myths

One important reason people fail at interviews is because of several misconceptions, or myths, about what really happens during the course of an interview. All of us know that the purpose of interviews is for an interviewer to hire someone who will perform well in a particular job, but beyond that few people fully grasp how interviews really work and what makes one candidate stand out more than another. This lack of understanding represents a major obstacle to maximising performance when sitting before an interviewer and trying to give your best answers. Interviews are no different to other endeavors in life: the better you understand how they work (or don't work), the higher the probability of tackling them successfully. An understanding of the underlying dynamics inherent in most interviews is an important start to improving your interview performance.

Myth no. 1: The best person for the job gets it

Sometimes this is true—especially in a situation where everyone knows everyone else, such as when a company is recruiting internally. However, this is often not the case. In order for the best person for the job to win it, a number of very important things need to be in place (and even then, there's no guarantee). These include:

- The interviewer knows what questions to ask and how to search for the truthfulness in answers. These two things may sound simple enough, but I can assure you that a large proportion of people conducting interviews have received no training, lack interview experience and often do not even go to the trouble of preparing for the interview.
- The interviewer is not taken in by the charm, good looks, great humour or any other aspect of the interviewee. This can be a difficult obstacle, even for experienced interviewers.
- The interviewee has learned how to clearly articulate their skills, key achievements and how they can add value to the organisation.
- There is no personality clash between interviewer and interviewee.
- Neither party is having a bad day.

Some employers—usually the ones who have been badly burnt by hiring the wrong people in the past—go to great lengths to set up professional hiring procedures designed to minimise hiring mistakes. Whilst some of these procedures are effective in improving candidate selection, they do not guarantee that the best person for the job will actually win it. In the final analysis, choosing someone for a job involves at least one human being making a decision about another, and no matter what we do to eliminate subjectivity, as human beings it is impossible to put aside our predispositions, predilections and personal preferences—no matter how much we may try to.

In an ideal world, the best person for the job would always win it; however, the reality is that it is often the person who performs best at the interview who wins the prize. The important lessons here are:

- Don't automatically pull out of applying for a job if you know someone better suited for the job is also applying for it. If you go to the trouble of preparing properly for the interview, there's a good chance that you may be seen as the preferred candidate—especially if the other person takes the interview for granted and fails to prepare.
- If you happen to know that you're the best person for the job, avoid taking the interview for granted. Behave as though you're

competing against formidable rivals. Take the time to prepare properly. Just because you've got a lot of experience does not mean you know how to convey this message at an interview.

Myth no. 2: Interviews are like school exams— the more you say, the better you'll do

Yes, interviews are a bit like exams in so far as that you're asked a number of questions to which you need to respond intelligently, but there the similarities end. Unlike exams, where lots of accurate detail is important, interviews are more about interacting and rapport building whilst simultaneously articulating smart answers. And a smart answer is often not the most detailed. In fact, long and overly detailed answers can drive interviewers to distraction, despite their technical accuracy. Knowing when to stop talking is a skill all successful interviewees have.

Also unlike many exams, there are often no right or wrong answers in interviews. We're all different and come to interviews from different backgrounds and business sitations. What is important at an interview is to justify your actions and talk about your achievements in a confident manner.

Myth no. 3: Interviewers know what they're doing

Some interviewers are very good at what they do, especially full-time professionals (provided they're not suffering from interview fatigue). However, many managers and owners of small businesses often flounder because interviewing is not something they do on a regular basis. Some sure signs of a bad interviewer are:

- *They* do most of the talking.
- They sound as though they've made up their mind about you in the first five minutes.
- They seem to pluck their questions randomly out of the ether.
- Their phone keeps ringing and they answer it.

- They sound like very sharp and less-than-honest salespeople when it comes to selling the job.

Some sure signs of a good interviewer are:

- They have their questions carefully prepared in advance.
- They want to know what you've done and how you've done it, including specific examples.
- They let *you* do most of the talking.
- They may want to interview you more than once.
- They will try to make you feel at ease.
- They are genuinely interested in your accomplishments, skills and the type of person you are.

Inexperienced interviewers generally don't ask the right questions and can easily be swayed by factors that have little to do with your ability to perform in the job. So if you are being interviewed by an inexperienced interviewer, don't wait to be asked a good question— one that will allow you to talk about all your wonderful skills and qualities. Rather, take the initiative in as unobtrusive a way as possible and talk about the things you feel the interviewer might really want to know. Unfortunately, this may not always be possible—especially if you're being interviewed by a forceful personality who loves the sound of their own voice. If ever you find yourself in such a situation, don't panic. Remind yourself that interviews are just as much about rapport-building as they are about answering questions. So nod your head, smile and make all the right noises—talkative interviewers love people who agree with them.

Myth no. 4: Never say 'I don't know'

Interviews are about making a positive impression by answering questions intelligently and building rapport with the interviewer. To this end, many interviewees feel that they have to provide the perfect answer to every question put to them, irrespective of whether or not they actually *know* the answer. Clearly, a great interview is one in which you can answer all the questions (and you should be able to do so if you take the time to prepare correctly); however, if you don't know the answer to something, it is better to admit to it rather than pretend to know and start waffling. Most interviewers can pick waffling a mile away and they don't like it for a couple of very important reasons: first, it is likely to make you sound dishonest; and second, it will make you sound considerably less than intelligent. You may as well not attend the interview if you give the impression that you're neither honest nor bright.

Trying to answer a question that you have little idea about could undermine an otherwise great interview. This does not mean that you cannot attempt answers that you are unsure of. There's nothing wrong with having a go, as long as you make your uncertainty clear to the interviewer at the outset. Here's what an answer may sound like:

> I have to be honest and say that this is not an area I'm familiar with, though I am very interested in it. If you like, I'm happy to have a go at trying to address the issue, as long as you're not expecting the perfect answer.

Or:

> I'd love to answer that question, but I need to be honest upfront and say that this is not an area that I'm overly familiar with, though I'm very interested in increasing my knowledge about it.

Myth no. 5: Good-looking people get the job

I suppose if the job was for a drop-dead gorgeous femme fatale type in a movie, then good looks would certainly help, but for most other jobs the way you look is not as big a deal as many people make out. As we've already discussed, there will always be an inexperienced employer who will hire on the basis of superficial factors, but most employers are smarter than that. The claim that good-looking people get the job over plain-looking people makes one seriously flawed assumption—that employers make a habit of putting someone's good looks before the interests of their livelihood. All my experience has taught me the contrary. Most businesses find themselves in highly competitive environments and employers are only too keenly aware that a poor hiring decision can prove very costly.

This is not to say that appearance and a bright personality are not important factors at an interview. It is very important that you dress appropriately and try your best to demonstrate all your friendly qualities. Good looks are certainly overrated in interviews, but an appropriate appearance and a friendly personality are not.

Myth no. 6: If you answer the questions better than the others, you'll get the job

Being able to articulate good answers in an interview is very important, and failure to do so will almost certainly mean you don't get the job. However, interviews—as we've already seen—are much more than just giving good answers. They're also about convincing the interviewer that you will be a nice person to work with. To put it another way, it doesn't matter how good your answers are technically, if the interviewer doesn't like you there's not much chance you'll get the job (unless your talents are unique, extremely difficult to find or the interviewer is desperate).

So avoid thinking about interviews just in terms of answering questions correctly. Interviews are also about establishing rapport and trust, and whilst there is no fail-safe method in doing this, there are things you can do (and things you should not do) that will go a long way towards improving your skills in this all-important area of interviewing.

Myth no. 7: You should try to give the perfect answer

I've heard too many people stumble over their words, repeat themselves and talk in circles because they're trying to articulate the perfect answer—or what they *think* constitutes the perfect answer. Some people are so obsessed with delivering the perfect answer that they don't stop until they produce what in their opinion is a word-perfect response.

Because we can never be entirely sure of what the interviewer wants to hear, some of us will keep on talking in the hope that we'll cover all bases. The problem with this approach is that we end up talking *too* much, leading to the interviewer losing concentration—which, of course, is the last thing you need at an interview. The reality is that in most cases there is no such thing as the perfect answer. The lesson here is: it makes a lot of sense to settle for a good answer that gets to the point rather than meander all over the place searching for the elusive perfect answer.

Myth no. 8: You must ask questions to demonstrate your interest and intelligence

Many interviewees are under the mistaken belief that they must ask questions at the end of the interview. There seems to be a common belief amongst many interviewees that this makes them sound more intelligent as well as more interested in the job. This is not true. Asking questions simply for the sake of doing so won't improve your chances of getting a job. It could even make you sound a little dull—especially if you ask questions about matters that were already covered during the course of the interview.

Only ask a question if you have a genuine query. Acceptable questions include those relating directly to the job you're applying for, as well as working conditions and company policies on such things as on pay, leave, and so on. Interviewers never mind answering questions about such matters, but they do mind answering questions they perceive to be irrelevant. If you have no questions to ask, simply say something like: 'Thankyou, but I have no questions. You've been very thorough during the course of the interview and have covered all the important matters regarding the job.' There's nothing wrong with including a compliment to the interviewer about their thoroughness and professionalism—provided it doesn't go over the top or sound like grovelling.

Two further points need to be made about asking questions. First, avoid asking too many questions. On the whole, interviewers do not enjoy role reversals. Second, never ask potentially embarrassing questions. These can include:

- a question relating to a negative incident;
- something that's not supposed to be in the public domain;
- a difficult question that may stump the interviewer.

The rule of thumb is: if you think a question may cause embarrassment, err on the side of caution and avoid it.

Myth no. 9: Relax and just be yourself

Whilst it is important to be relaxed and show your better side, it is also very important to understand that interviews are not social engagements. Most interviews are highly formalised events in which otherwise innocuous behaviours are deemed unacceptable. In short, being your usual self could spell disaster (as contradictory as that may sound). For example, if being yourself means leaning back on your chair, dressing somewhat shabbily and making jokes, you might find yourself attending an inordinate number of interviews. Whilst interviewers like people to be relaxed, they also have definite expectations about what behaviours are appropriate for an interview—and you violate these expectations at your peril!

Myth no. 10: Interviewers are looking for flaws

The danger with this myth is that it can easily lead to interviewees adopting a defensive, perhaps even distrustful, attitude during the interview. If you believe that the interviewer is assiduously searching for your flaws, it will more than likely undermine your attempts to establish that all-important rapport and trust. It may also prevent you from opening up and giving really good answers. Rest assured that most interviewers do not prepare their interview questions with a view to uncovering your flaws. Questions are mostly prepared with a view to giving the interviewer an overall or holistic insight into what you have to offer the company. A good interviewer will indeed uncover areas in which you are not strong, but that is a far cry from thinking that the interviewer is hell bent on uncovering only your flaws.

It is very important to treat every question as an opportunity to excel rather than being unnecessarily guarded. It is only by answering the questions that you can demonstrate how good you are. To treat questions as objects of suspicion makes no sense at all.

Understanding the myths surrounding interviews gives you a great start for success. Remember, interviews are no different to other endeavors in life: the better you understand their underlying nature the higher the probability you'll tackle them successfully. An insight into common interview myths will arm you with the information you need to prevent you from falling into those disheartening traps. Just as importantly, a clearer picture of the true nature of interviews better informs the rest of your preparation and will contribute to your confidence and performance.

Summary of key points

- The best person for the job does not necessarily win it—often it's the person who gives the best interview.
- Interviews are more than just giving technically correct answers. They're also very much about building rapport.
- Not all interviewers know what they're doing; your job is to know how to handle the good and bad interviewer.
- It's better to be honest and admit ignorance than try to pretend you know an answer and come across as disingenuous and less than bright.
- Good looking people win jobs—maybe in Hollywood movies, but on the whole, employers are keen to hire talent over superficial factors.
- Striving to give the perfect answer can get you into trouble. It's better

to give a good answer that's to the point rather than searching for perfection; besides, often there's no such thing as the perfect answer.

- Do not ask questions for the sake of it. Only ask a question if you have a genuine query that has not been covered.
- Interviews are formal occasions requiring relatively formal behaviours. Interviewers will expect this and may react negatively if they don't see it.
- Interviewers do not spend all their time looking for your flaws. They're more interested in getting an overall picture of who you are. Avoid answering questions defensively. It's much better to see every question as an opportunity to highlight your best points.

2 Convincing them you're **right** for the job

Doing well at interviews is not nearly as difficult as many people think. With correct preparation and a little practice, most people who dread interviews can learn to excel. The important thing to note is that performing well at interviews is a *learned* process. Highly effective interviewees are not born with interview skills; rather, they teach themselves what to say, how to say it and how to behave during an interview.

Common interview mistakes

All of us have made mistakes during interviews, and most of us have walked out of interviews thinking of all the great things we forgot to mention and all the things we shouldn't have said. But the most important thing about mistakes is learning from them—and not repeating them. Here are some common interview mistakes:

- *Failing to express oneself clearly.* Often, because of anxiety and wanting to say things perfectly, we try too hard and turn what should be simple sentences into convoluted nonsense. Simple language is always the most effective. Avoid trying to sound knowledgeable by using jargon or complex sentences.
- *Not being aware of one's body language.* Many interviewees succeed in alienating the interviewer because they pay little or no

attention to their body language. Body language is an extremely powerful communicator, and failing to use it effectively will almost certainly put you at a significant disadvantage. Eye contact, sitting position and facial expressions are all very important aspects of interviewing, and need to be thought through before the interview.

- *Failing to control those nerves.* Sometimes people allow their nerves to get so out of control that they fail to establish rapport and even forget their answers. Feeling anxious before and during an interview is common. In fact, a touch of nerves can be a good thing. But there is no need to be the victim of debilitating nerves. As you read through this book, you'll gradually learn how to lessen your anxiety.
- *Failing to give appropriate examples.* Failing to give examples, or giving inappropriate examples, will spell disaster. Before the interview, it is important to think of relevant examples of what you've achieved and how you went about realising those achievements. Saying that you achieved something without being able to back it up with specific examples will only get you a rejection letter. Your examples need to be easy to understand, follow a logical sequence and be relevant to the needs of the employer. None of this happens without preparation.
- *Trying too hard to please the interviewer.* Whilst building rapport and trust during the interview is critical, few interviewers appreciate interviewees going overboard with their behaviour. Obsequious behaviours are generally seen as a form of deceit and carry little weight—in fact, they can undermine your efforts to create trust.

There's nothing wrong with you

You've probably committed at least some of the mistakes listed above. It's very important to realise that making such mistakes is common. In other words, *there's nothing wrong with you*. In the vast majority of cases, performing poorly at an interview happens because of the very nature of interviews—it's the interview process that is the culprit.

So an awareness of the basic nature of interviews is the first step in a step-by-step process by which you can significantly improve your performance. A great place to start is to ask: 'What does it take to convince the interviewer that you're the best person for the job?'

The answer to this question can best be summarised in four parts:

- correct preparation;
- knowing the things that are important to interviewers;
- practising your answers;
- perseverance.

Correct preparation

How well you perform at an interview will largely depend on how well you have prepared for it. Failure to correctly prepare almost certainly means you will not perform at your best. In some cases, it will mean performing quite badly, which may contribute to the erosion of your confidence.

Even if you're lucky enough to be the favoured candidate, and are almost certain to win the position by just turning up, you should still take the time to prepare because the better you perform, the greater the likelihood that you will negotiate a better salary—and often the difference in money can be substantial.

We've all heard people boast that they've never prepared for an interview in their lives and have done all right. Whilst this boast may not be an idle one, closer inspection will usually reveal that these people were:

- lucky—that is, in the right place at the right time;
- well connected;
- working in a favourable labour market where there was a huge demand for employees coupled with low supply;
- applying for jobs well within their comfort zone—that is, not stretching themselves to improve their position; or

- applying for jobs internally and competing mainly against external candidates.

The case for preparation

The argument for interview preparation becomes compelling when you give some thought to the basic nature of interviews. Not only are you expected to sell yourself in a competitive environment, but you're also expected to compress large and often complex pieces of information into neat and highly articulate answers that avoid any negative connotations and contain the information the interviewer wants to hear. It's no wonder people's stress levels increase. But it doesn't end there. There are three additional reasons that make the case for interview preparation even more compelling:

- Interviews are rare events, thus making them unfamiliar and awkward.
- Many people find it very difficult to sell themselves at interviews because they've been conditioned by family and society not to blow their own trumpet. Making simple statements such as 'I am very good at selling xyz' can be quite an obstacle to overcome.
- In most interviews, coming second isn't good enough. It's not just a matter of performing well; it's also a matter of beating everyone else.

It is unimaginable that you would fail to prepare for an event that is infrequent, competitive and requires behaviours not normally used. Yet that is exactly what people do when they walk into an interview without preparation.

What is incorrect preparation?

Incorrect preparation is any preparation that will not optimise your performance at an interview. Rote-learning generic answers that someone else has prepared has limited value. At best, they can give you an insight into what may constitute a good answer; at worst, they simply lead you astray. It is important to understand that, in the vast majority of cases, there's no such thing as a single answer to a question. What may constitute a great answer for one employer may be viewed as quite ordinary by another. One of the worst things you can do is learn other people's responses off by heart and repeat them at an interview. Repeating other people's so-called great answers can make you sound disingenuous and make you look a bit ridiculous when asked a probing follow up question. It makes a lot more sense to prepare your own answers.

Advantages of preparation

Taking the time to correctly prepare for an interview will:

- improve your confidence levels;
- assist you in answering questions succinctly, as opposed to taking forever to make a simple point;
- help you know what to say and how to say it;
- assist you in handling difficult questions;
- help you avoid saying things that will make a negative impression;
- improve your rapport-building skills.

Knowing the things that are important to interviewers

One of the keys to knowing what to prepare lies in understanding the needs of the interviewer. Once you know the things that are important to interviewers, interview preparation suddenly becomes a lot clearer and a lot more manageable.

The vast majority of interviewers—whether or not they realise it—want to hear three things from you. In fact, nearly all good interview questions boil down to these three key generic questions:

- *Can you do the job?* In other words, do you have the skills, knowledge, experience or potential to perform well in the job? Most interviewers will spend the majority of the interview probing you on this question. They'll want to know what you've done, how you did it and what the outcomes were. In the event you have not performed a particular duty, they will try to ascertain your potential to do the job.

- *Are you the sort of person they can work with?* Another way of stating this question is: Will you fit into the existing culture of the organisation? Or, in the case of small organisations: Will you get on with the boss? Whilst interviewers generally spend a lot less time on this question, it is nevertheless a vitally important one—that's because no one wants to work with someone they don't like, even if they can do the job.
- *How motivated are you?* In other words, what energy levels and drive do you bring to the position? You may not even be asked a question about your motivation levels, but you fail to address it at your peril. As we all know, highly motivated employees are keenly sought after by employers—with good reason.

There are two significant benefits in knowing that interviewers are keenly interested in these three generic questions, and that the vast majority of questions they can ask fall under one or more of these categories. First, it guides you in the preparation of your answers (a large part of this book is based on answering these three key questions). Rather than spending lots of time wading through randomly selected questions in the hope that you will have prepared the right answers, an understanding of the significance of the three key generic questions provides a direction and platform for your preparation. In short, you are able to plan your preparation around the following issues:

- your skills, knowledge and experience—*can you do the job?* (see Chapters 3, 4 and 5);
- your personal attributes—*are you the sort of person they can work with?* (see Chapter 6);
- your motivation levels (see Chapter 7).

Second, it provides a useful way to deal with questions at the actual interview. By sorting interview questions into one or more of the three generic question categories, your answers will gain added structure and a clearer direction simply because you know what the underlying purpose of the questions is. By learning how to recognise the real intent of a question, you minimise your chances of giving the wrong answer and/or waffling.

Practice

The third aspect of convincing an interviewer that you're the best person for the job is practice. Unfortunately, there are no shortcuts to developing great interview skills. Once you've prepared your answers, you need to sit down and practise them as much as you can. The more you practise, the better you'll be. As the old saying goes, 'success is one part talent and nine parts perseverance'. How you practise is up to you. Do it in front of the mirror, sitting on your couch, pacing your room or while driving your car—but avoid practising in front of your boss!

Practising your answers aloud

It is important to practise your answers aloud, rather than just mentally rehearsing them. That's because the human brain distinguishes between talking and thinking and you need to stimulate the talking part of your brain. Thinking your answers at an interview will get you nowhere, unless the interviewer is a mind reader.

Get some feedback

Ideally, you should do your practising at real interviews. The more interviews you attend, the better—even if you have to attend interviews for jobs that you're not really interested in. After the interview—assuming you're not the winning candidate—ring back the interviewer and ask for feedback on your performance. Some interviewers are happy to provide this feedback; however, many prefer not to because they find it threatening and a waste of their time. These people will either avoid you altogether or provide you with such watered-down feedback that it will be virtually useless.

In some instances you may not be able to resolve this problem; however, you can increase your chances of getting honest feedback by making interviewers feel as comfortable as possible. You can do this by a) assuring them that you only want five minutes of their time; and b) telling them that the only reason you're seeking feedback is to improve future interview performance.

Mock interviews

If you cannot get yourself to as many interviews as you would like, it's a good idea to set up mock interviews with someone you can work with. The more closely you can simulate a real-life situation, more benefit you will derive. An effective way to conduct mock interviews is to get into role and stay in it for the entire interview. No distractions, no small talk and especially no starting again. If possible, avoid providing the questions to your helpers—let them come up with their own. If your helpers are not in a position to do this, give them lots of questions and ask them to choose the ones they want. The important thing for you is to get yourself used to answering *unexpected* questions. Furthermore, if you feel your helper can provide you with *honest* feedback on your performance, do not shy away from asking. You never know what you may learn. Often it's the small things that make a big difference. But be on your guard for overly positive feedback. Chances are that your helper will be a friend, and friends are well known for avoiding negatives.

Perseverance

The worst thing you can do when setting out to improve your interview performance is give up because it all seems too hard. Quitters invariably get nowhere. They certainly don't land great jobs and build great careers. On the other hand, people who persevere very often gain valuable insights simply because they have the stamina to stick it out.

The people we admire most are often those who face seemingly insurmountable obstacles yet instead of quitting, quietly resolve to overcome them. On the other side of the coin, the people we generally least respect are those who are forever starting things without finishing them. They tend to be the same people who make grandiose claims but end up delivering little or nothing. One common characteristic that chronic quitters tend to have is low self-esteem—they don't really believe in themselves. And if you don't believe in yourself, others usually don't believe in you either—not a great place to be when you're trying to convince interviewers to believe in your abilities. These are the people who are often heard saying things such as: 'That's too hard', 'I can't learn that', 'What will others think', etc. They also tend to be the people who are always complaining about things but never seem to take any action to correct them because there's always an excuse.

You don't have to be a chronic quitter or burdened with low self-esteem to give up on working on your interview skills—there could be any number of other reasons. However, if you're reading this book there's a good chance that improving your interview skills is an important priority in your life, and therefore should not be let go easily. If you feel you might be one of those people who is standing on the precipice of quitting, here is a little exercise that can assist you to take a step or two back from the edge.

Suggested activity: Neurolinguistic programming

Based on neurolinguistic programming (NLP), this exercise is designed to influence how you feel. People often quit because they associate negative feelings with what they're doing. People who persevere have the power to feel good about their actions no matter how tedious or unconstructive these actions may seem to others. If you can make yourself feel good about the process of improving your interview skills, then there's a good chance that quitting will be the last thing on your mind. Next time you feel like quitting, you might like to find a quiet spot and take the following steps:

- Close your eyes and imagine yourself performing extremely well in an interview. Take your time to view this picture in as much detail as you can. Picture the faces of the enthusiastic interviewers, noticing how attentive they are and how impressed they are with your responses. Immerse yourself in the experience. Pay attention to the details, including sounds, smells, colours, temperature, and so on. Above all, capture the feeling of being successful. Do not hold yourself back. The better you make yourself feel, the more powerful the exercise will be.

- Keep on repeating this exercise until you capture that feeling of excitement. You may be able to generate greater excitement by picturing yourself in your new job. Imagine how good it is going to feel winning a great job. Imagine getting that all important phone call informing you of your success. Picture yourself in the position doing all those things you've dreamt of doing. The key to this exercise is to generate the great feeling that goes with succeeding at an interview. Your only limitation is your imagination.

- Once you've captured that feeling, the next step is to recreate it when you need it—in other words, when you feel like quitting. An effective way of recreating the feeling of excitement is by installing what NLP refers to as an *anchor*. An anchor is a stimulus that triggers the desired feelings when you want them. An anchor can be something you do, say or imagine. Action anchors usually work best. For example, you might cross your fingers or jump up in the air or pull your ears. It doesn't matter what it is, as long as you can do it easily when you want to and trigger the desired feelings. Every time you're afflicted with the scourge of quitting, use your anchor and let your ability to influence your feelings do the rest.

Summary of key points

- Because of their nature, interviews are inherently challenging. Making mistakes at an interview is something that everyone does. The good news is that we can overcome our errors by correct preparation, practice and perseverance.

- Beware of faulty preparation. Avoid rote learning of other people's answers. Always prepare your own.
- Knowing what employers want to hear at an interview constitutes a great start for preparing your own answers and simplifies interview preparation. What most employers want to hear can be represented by three key questions:
  - Can you do the job?
  - Are you the sort of person they can work with?
  - How motivated are you?
- Get in as much practice as you can and always ask for *honest* feedback.
- Perseverance is everything.
- Banish all thoughts of quitting by teaching yourself to associate strong feelings of excitement with improving your interview skills.

3 Can you do the job?

Before an employer decides to give someone a job, they need to be convinced that the person can either do the job properly or learn it quickly. It comes as no surprise to learn therefore that 'Can you do the job?' questions are the most common. They're also the ones people spend most time preparing for.

'Can you do the job?' questions are those that directly or indirectly seek to ascertain your ability to perform the duties inherent in a job. They include questions that seek to clarify your:

- skills;
- knowledge;
- experience;
- key achievements;
- potential performance.

Examples of 'Can you do the job?' questions include:

- Can you give us an example of a time you had to communicate something that was complex and controversial? How did you go about it?
- Tell us about one of your key achievements?
- An irate client rings and gives you a blast over the phone. How do you handle it?
- What do you think you can bring to this position?

- Can you give us an example of a project that you had to plan and organise? What steps did you take?
- How would you describe yourself? (At first glance this may not strike you as a 'Can you do the job?' question, but effective interviewees always look for ways to highlight their skills.)
- What would you say makes an effective manager of people?
- Why should we employ you?
- What do you regard as your greatest strength?
- The most important duty in your job will be to look after the x, y and z. Tell us how you intend going about it.

Three types of 'Can you do the job?' questions

Unless you're being interviewed for a job that's almost identical to one you've already had, it is likely that you will be asked three types of 'Can you do the job?' questions. These are:

- questions about duties that you have performed before (see Chapter 3);
- questions about duties that you have not performed but whose skills you have mastered (see Chapter 4);
- questions about duties that are entirely new to you (see Chapter 5).

Finding out as much about the job as possible

The first thing you need to do is take a very close look at the duties and requirements of the job you're applying for. It is these duties and requirements that will form the basis of your answers. There are several ways of collecting this sort of information:

- scrutinising the job advertisement;
- accessing a duty statement—if there is one;
- contacting the employer or recruitment agent to clarify the main responsibilities of the job.

In an ideal world, you would have access to a detailed job advertisement, an up-to-date duty statement and an employer happy to discuss the main responsibilities of the job. Unfortunately, all too often the reality is that job ads are thinly worded, duty statements are non-existent and employers do not have time to return your calls. However, it is critical that you find out as much about the job as possible before sitting down and thinking about your answers. The best source of information is either the employer or the recruitment agent. Job ads and duty statements are useful (sometimes they're all that you will have); however, duty statements can often be out of date and job ads can lack sufficient information.

Talking to the right people can provide you with insights that often cannot be picked up from the written word. You might find out, for example, that the position you're applying for was made vacant because the previous incumbent had poor interpersonal communication skills and became aggressive when anyone expressed a differing opinion. In such a case, it is likely that the employer will be looking for a replacement with excellent interpersonal communication and team player skills. You'd have a far better chance of winning the job if you had accessed this information before the interview and taken the time to prepare your answers.

Talking to an employer to find out more

If you're able to talk to the employer, *be sure you've got your questions prepared*. The last thing you want to do is waste their time by stumbling through poorly thought-out questions. If the employer does not return your call, do not throw in the towel. Often the person who answers the phone can be an invaluable source of information—especially in small to medium sized enterprises. There's a good chance that they know a great deal about the position, or they might know someone else who does and is willing to talk to you. Here are some useful rules when talking to an employer before the interview:

- Avoid small talk and get straight to the point. Small talk will be seen as sucking up—which, of course, it is!
- Avoid asking too many questions—just ask the important ones, unless the employer has made it obvious that they've got lots of time on their hands and is willing to talk to you.
- Never ask frivolous questions—those that can be answered from the advertisement or that a good applicant would be expected to know the answers to.
- Where necessary, provide a succinct reason why you're asking the question—the employer may not understand the significance of the question and could draw the wrong conclusions.
- Thank them for their time and tell them you're looking forward to the interview.

A quick word about duty statements

Duty statements are simply a summary of the main duties of a job. Whilst they're a great source of information, they can be out of date. So, if you've been sent one, make the effort to find out whether the information on it is still valid. Checking on a duty statement can represent a great opportunity to contact the employer and ask a few questions. Unfortunately, duty statements are usually the preserve of large organisations. Smaller companies generally lack the resources to write them.

Gleaning information from a job advertisement

When you scrutinise the job advertisement, make a list of all the duties/requirements associated with the position. The idea is to try to read between the lines as much as possible. The more duties and requirements you come up with, the more thorough your preparation will be, which will lessen the chances of being caught unprepared at the interview.

The four steps to interview success

The four steps to interview success are designed to capture all the relevant information you need to construct interview answers within a simple-to-manage framework. This method features four columns, with the headings shown below in Table 3.1.

Table 3.1 The four steps to interview success

Step 1	Step 2	Step 3	Step 4
Duties/requirements of the position I'm applying for	What I've already done that relates directly to the duties listed in step 1, including overcoming obstacles	Current or past context	Outcomes—organisational and personal

By filling out each of the columns in the table, you are effectively collecting all the information you'll need to answer a broad range of questions. Most importantly, it's *your relevant* information, not information gathered from other people's answers you've read elsewhere. Once you've captured the required information, your next step is to put it together in response to a range of likely interview questions and then practise your answers.

Behavioural questions

One of the key advantages of the four steps method is that it lends itself to addressing a popular questioning technique commonly referred to as *behavioural questioning*. You can recognise one of these questions every time an interviewer asks you for specific examples to back up a claim you have made, including the steps you took and the obstacles you encountered. Behavioural questions are designed to uncover the actions (behaviours) behind an outcome or a duty, and cannot be successfully answered without preparing the third column.

If you're a graduate or a new entrant to the workforce, there's still a good chance that you will be asked behavioural questions; however, they will be limited in scope. Instead of asking for employment-related experience, interviewers will ask for study- or life-related incidences. For example, the interviewer may want to know how well you function in a team, so may ask you about the last time you had to complete an assignment with a group of students. The same principle applies to communication skills, planning and organising, conflict resolution, your ability to cope with change, and so on.

Using the four steps

Once you've come up with as much information as you can about the job, you need to start thinking about preparing your answers regarding duties you've performed before. All you need to do is recount your past actions and achievements and link them to the new job.

But be careful not to take these interviews for granted. It is all too easy to fall into the trap of not preparing because you think that the questions will be easy. However, just because you've performed the same duties does not mean you will be able to articulate the details of what you did and how you did it. There's a big difference between doing something and actually having to talk about it in a succinct and coherent fashion.

Your first step is to select all the duties/requirements of the new job that you have performed before and recount your past actions and achievements in a way that will make the creation of effective answers easy. Use Table 3.1 to capture all the information you will need, including what you did, how you did it, the context in which you did it and the outcomes. A more detailed explanation of each of the steps, including what to include and not include in each column, follows.

Step1: Duties or requirements

List the duties and requirements of the job you're applying for in the first column.

Step 2: What you did and how you did it

The second column (step 2) contains the core of your answers, including the obstacles you overcame to satisfy the duties or requirements listed in step 1. When filling out this column, avoid writing broad-ranging or general answers, though this may not always be possible. The idea is to break up the duty or requirement listed in step 1 into its primary tasks or components. It helps if you ask yourself the following question: In order to complete the duty or requirement in step 1, what individual actions did I take, including any actions I took to overcome obstacles? Then list these in a logical sequence.

Avoid rushing through this step, especially if it has been a while since you've performed a particular duty. A good idea is to write all the things you can think of and then reduce the list down to the key points. Include specific examples.

Be careful not to over-elaborate when filling out the second column. Doing so can inadvertently lead to answers containing far too much detail. Given that many interviewees feel they have to show off their hard-earned knowledge, it is easy to go overboard in step 2. But, in the vast majority of cases, you are not required to cover every contingency when answering a question. Try to avoid talking for longer than you should, thus boring the interviewer. Most interviewers are able to draw sensible inferences from the main points in your answer. If they want more information, they'll ask for it.

If you do have lots of great information that you absolutely feel cannot be left out, then go ahead and list them in the second column, but be selective about what you use at the interview. Only choose the most relevant points. You can leave your other points for other questions or, if there are no follow-up questions, pat yourself on the back for being thorough in your preparation.

Not providing exhaustive answers at an interview makes a lot of sense when you factor in the importance of rapport-building during the course of an interview. Remember: *building rapport with the interviewer is the most important thing you can do at an interview and talking too much works against that all-important goal.*

How long should my answers be?

Some answers can be as short as one word; others may run into many sentences. It all depends on the question and the circumstances. Here are some helpful guidelines on keeping your answers within acceptable parameters.

Let's make some reasonable assumptions. Say your interview will run for 40 minutes. Take away five minutes for settling and the exchange of pleasantries. That leaves you about 35 minutes. (It never hurts to ask how long the interview will run, but ask *before* the interview, not at the actual interview, lest you give the impression that you're in a hurry to be somewhere else.) Now, let's say the job contains ten main duties and requirements and that the interviewer has prepared two questions per primary duty/requirement. That means you have to answer, at a minimum, twenty questions within 35 minutes, which means you'll have a little under two minutes per question. This does not mean that you set your timer at one minute and fifty seconds for every question—it simply means that it is reasonable to assume the interviewers have left a little less than two minutes to get through their primary questions.

However, it is also reasonable to assume that the interviewer may want to spend more time on particular questions. If you've done your homework, there's a good chance that you'll know beforehand which questions the interviewers will wish to spend a little extra time on. If not, it's up to you to be as alert as possible during the interview. Look out for any clues (such as body language and tone of voice) that may indicate the interviewer is placing extra importance on particular questions. The point is that it's OK to spend a little extra time on these sorts of questions.

Avoid subjective or liberal interpretations of questions. Listen very carefully to the question, and *answer it*. This sounds obvious, but people do have a bad habit of assuming that the interviewer is wanting to hear a whole lot of other things. Just stick to the question. If interviewers have other questions, there's a good chance they'll ask them.

Step 3: Context

Once you've listed what you did and how you did it under step 2, it is important to give some thought to the *context* or *situation* in which you did it. Without context, your answers will sound empty or only half-completed. In fact, as we shall see a little later, it is often a good idea to *begin your answers* by giving the interviewer an insight into the context in which you performed the duties. For example, it's better to start an answer by saying, 'I planned and organised my work in a fast-paced entrepreneurial environment where clients wanted everything in a big hurry', rather than saying, 'I planned and organised my work by ensuring that my work schedule took upcoming events into account'. Whilst there's nothing wrong with the latter, the former is a better beginning because it *sets the scene* and gives the interviewer a better *insight into the environment* in which you worked.

By talking about context, you're giving the interviewer a better appreciation of the work you did, as well as its relevance to the job you're applying for. Without a clearly articulated context, your answers will consist of little more than a bunch of tasks you completed. And there's a good chance interviewers will adopt one of those indifferent expressions indicating that, no matter what you say thereafter, they have decided you're not getting the job.

Please note that you only need to establish context once for each job you did. Repeating context for the same job is nonsensical and is likely to make the interviewer think that you bumped your head against something hard on your way to the interview!

Step 4: Outcomes

This step involves writing down the key outcomes or results of your actions. One of the things I've noticed over the years is that many people find it difficult to articulate the good things that have resulted from their work. When I ask them why, I soon discover it's because many of them don't think in terms of outcomes. Unfortunately, their thinking is primarily confined to what they did, and sometimes how they did it. However, outcomes or achievements are arguably the most important aspect of your work. There's little point in doing all the right things if you don't achieve any positive outcomes. From an interviewer's point of view, outcomes are critical.

When thinking about outcomes, it is useful to separate them into *organisation* and *personal* categories.

Organisational outcomes

Organisational outcomes include any improvements accrued by the organisation as a result of your work. Sometimes these are easy to quantify, especially if you've been involved in making, selling, installing or changing something. When thinking about organisational outcomes, many people confine themselves to the *evident outcomes*— or the things they actually *did*. Examples of evident outcomes include such things as implementing a new filing system, changing report templates or building a new database for keeping track of customer contacts. Needless to say, it is important to mention these outcomes at an interview. However, the shortfall with evident outcomes is that they fail to articulate their primary benefits to the organisation. Saying you implemented a new filing system is great, but your answer would be much better if you also articulated the benefit of this new filing system to the employer. For example:

- Productivity rose by 5 per cent.
- Quality of service, as measured by customer feedback, improved significantly.
- Customer service levels improved by 12 per cent.
- Staff satisfaction and moral improved by over 8 per cent.
- Turn-around times nearly halved.

'Best guess' estimates are fine in this situation.

You will have noticed that most of the above outcomes are *quantified*. In general, quantified outcomes sound a lot more credible than just saying something 'improved'. However, if you do not have specific numbers to talk about, approximations will do—providing you can back them up. Unfortunately, many interviewees feel they cannot talk about the specific improvements their efforts led to because they worked for an organisation that did not measure outcomes. If you find yourself in this situation, you should not allow your employer's failure to measure to deter you from articulating 'best guess' improvements. You are entitled to say to the interviewer that, even though the benefits to the organisation were not measured, you estimate that improvements were in the range of x per cent. But be warned—do not go making over-inflated claims, otherwise you'll lose credibility. And be sure you can justify your 'best guess' claims.

Here are some phrases that may assist you in articulating outcomes that were not measured:

- Anecdotal evidence strongly indicated . . .
- All the feedback we received showed that . . .
- The stakeholders were unanimous in their praise.
- Senior management felt that the goals were more than met.
- Judging by the time saved, we estimated that productivity improved by . . .

Here's an example of an answer that includes employer benefit outcomes that were not measured:

As result of the new filing system, time spent by staff locating certain documents decreased significantly, which gave them more time to concentrate on other work. Even though we did not measure precisely how much time was saved, the feedback I received from the users strongly indicated that productivity improved by at least 5 per cent.

Personal outcomes
In their rush to talk about organisational outcomes, interviewees often neglect to talk about their personal outcomes. Articulating personal outcomes can be a very effective interview technique, particularly when those outcomes are directly relevant to the job you're applying for. It's also an effective way to highlight an important skill or insight to an interviewer who seems to be incapable of asking appropriate questions.

Personal outcomes include any benefits *you* have accrued as a result of your work. These can include:

- learning new skills;
- improving existing skills;
- gaining new insights;
- various forms of recognition, including promotion or monetary gain.

For example, stating that, at the end of a big project, you felt a wonderful sense of accomplishment (a very natural thing to feel) signals to the interviewer that you're the sort of person who is motivated by working on and successfully completing a large project. Here are some examples of simple but effective personal outcome endings:

As a result of working on the project, my planning and organisational skills improved dramatically. (skills-based)

By the end of my stay with company x, my insight into the legal aspects of occupational health and safety requirements had improved significantly. (knowledge-based)

One of the pleasing things about working with the project team was discovering how much I enjoyed working in a team environment. I always thought that I functioned better working solo, but I discovered that I was highly effective working as part of a team. (skills-based and motivation relating to teamwork)

Suggested activity: Personal outcomes

Before you go on, see whether you can come up with three personal outcome endings of your own.

Putting it all altogether

Having created your answers, you need to bring together the information you've captured in the four steps in order to construct answers that can be used to tackle a broad range of relevant questions. One of the main advantages of using the four steps is that you can easily construct answers that address a range of questions relating to the duties and requirements in step 1. Here are some important tips to help you construct an answer.

Posing questions to yourself

The first thing to do is pose a question relating to the duty or requirement listed under step 1. Start off with a question that you feel comfortable with, then answer it using the information in the other three columns. At the start, it is a good idea to write your answers down. This will give you some all-important structure and direction. However, committing answers to paper does not imply that you have to memorise them word for word. In fact, doing so can be counter-productive—for two reasons. First, precise word-for-word answers are suited to highly specific questions, and there is no guarantee that you will be asked the specific question you've prepared for. Second, memorising answers to such a degree can rob you of two of the most important skills used in interviews: flexibility and an ability to think on your feet. The important thing is to *memorise the main points of your answers*. You are not required to regurgitate them in exactly the same order using exactly the same sentences.

Once you've written your answer down and practised it to the point where you've achieved a satisfactory level of fluency (without referring to your notes), you can ask and answer other questions relating to the same duty or requirement. Two to three questions for each of the duties/requirements under step 1 should suffice. You can do more if you choose; however, you'll probably find that, with more questions, you'll be repeating your answers.

How to pose your own questions

Generating your own questions is a simple process if you tackle it from the perspective of the interviewer. Put yourself in the shoes of the interviewer and ask yourself what questions you would need to ask to ascertain whether the interviewee could perform the relevant duty or job requirement. You will need to take into account behavioural questioning techniques, which are designed to uncover the specific actions behind stated claims. An example of a behavioural-based question relating to working in an entrepreneurial environment is: 'Tell us about the way you dealt with working in a fast-paced entrepreneurial environment. What steps or techniques worked for you?' Notice the key phrases: 'the way you dealt with' and 'What steps or techniques worked for you?' This question is trying to uncover the key behaviours underpinning successful work in an entrepreneurial environment.

By asking yourself such questions, there is a good chance that you will come close to anticipating the interview questions—or at least be more precise about the intent of the interview questions. The actual question at the interview probably will sound different to the question you posed yourself, but its intent or purpose will be similar. In other words, even though questions may be worded differently, the content of your answers should be relevant to the interview.

Where possible begin your answer with the context (see step 3). Think of context as the foundation upon which you build some of your answers. The clearer the context, the more sense the rest of your answer will make to the interviewer. The interviewer will know what sort of environment you were working in and how important your duties were to the success of the job, not to mention your own employment.

Once you've established context in one question you do not have to keep on mentioning the same context for every question relating to the same workplace. Only mention context again if a new one is being discussed.

What you did and how you did it

Once you've established context, you're free to launch into the heart of your answer: the specifics of what you did and how you did it (see step 2).

Finishing your answer with an outcome or outcomes

As much as possible, try to conclude with a positive outcome.
Summarising the above points, here's what a question and a full
answer might sound like:

> **Question:** *Tell us about the way you dealt with working in a fast-
> paced entrepreneurial environment.*
>
> Whilst working for this company, an important client needed
> changes made to one of the orders she had placed and she
> needed these changes completed within a very short space
> of time. Given that a number of our clients worked in un-
> predictable environments, these requests were not uncommon.
> Our job was to ensure that we could meet them, otherwise
> we'd effectively be out of a job.

This establishes the context—step 3. Amongst other things, this
opening tells the interviewer about the significance of your work.

> The way I dealt with working in such a demanding environ-
> ment was to ensure that my planning took into account the
> fact that matters could change at any minute. For example,
> I made it very clear to my clients and colleagues that, due to
> the nature of my work, I might be changing appointments
> or sending someone else instead of myself. I also avoided
> making long-term commitments. Coping in such a hectic
> environment also meant that I had to make some fundamental
> changes in the way I thought about work. I had to quickly
> jettison the idea of working predictable hours and performing
> foreseeable tasks. I also had to come to terms with the idea
> that work can often be unpredictable requiring a great deal
> of flexibility. Now I could never see myself going back to a
> settled working environment.
>
> I also had to be prepared to learn new things quickly as
> the need arose. For this job, I had to learn the basics of
> PowerPoint and Access in a few days and apply them on the
> job. Retraining becomes a way of life, as does learning to
> work well with others.

This reflects step 2: what you did and how you did it. The answer clearly and succinctly states what actions were taken (planning), and gives specific examples of *how* they were taken (e.g changing appointments).

> The outcomes of my work were very motivating for me. Not only did we consistently meet the client's requests, but we had an excellent record in terms of our customer service levels as measured by our twice yearly customer service survey.

This is an illustration of step 4: outcomes. In this case, two organisational outcomes have been stated: 'consistently met client's requests' and 'excellent customer service'. And there is one personal outcome—'high levels of motivation'.

This answer is a thorough one, and you would probably not use all of it in response to a single question. However, thorough preparation is a wise precaution. You may choose to use only a part of this answer in response to a team player question and keep the rest in reserve for another team player question or a question requiring similar skills. Feel free to 'cut and paste' your answers as the need arises.

The elements of a good interview response contained in this answer include the following:

- It provided specific examples.
- It mentioned learning the basics of PowerPoint and Access.
- It stated what you did and how you did it—for example, changing appointments; avoiding making long-term commitments; learning new things quickly as the need arose; retraining; and letting go of the idea that work is predictable and inflexible.
- It stated outcomes and mentioned being motivated by outcomes, including consistently meeting clients' requests and an excellent record in terms of customer service levels.
- It avoided meandering all over the place.

One of the strengths of the four steps is that we can answer a range of questions relating to the duty or requirement under step 1. Below are responses to some other questions relating to working in an entrepreneurial environment.

Question: *Which part of working in an entrepreneurial environment did you find most challenging?*
Given the short time frames and levels of work required, the most challenging aspect for me—at least in the beginning—was meeting the client's tight deadlines. (step 3).

I met this challenge by improving the way I planned for contingencies, by training myself in several software packages including PowerPoint and Access, and by putting into place measures that improved the communication amongst key stakeholders. (step 2).

The outcomes were very positive. Not only did I begin to meet the client's deadlines, but I also put into place communication procedures that improved organisational efficiency. (step 4).

Question: *What did you enjoy most about working in an entrepreneurial environment?*
The part I enjoyed most was meeting the tight deadlines set by the clients. I always felt a deep sense of satisfaction every time we successfully overcame a difficult challenge (step 4).

A lot of planning and well-organised work needed to be completed before the deadlines were successfully met. (steps 2 and 3). For example, we needed to ensure that all members of the team were continually communicating with one another and that everyone had the required training. I enjoyed working in a fast-paced and challenging environment which stretched me on a daily basis.

Question: *How do you manage the pressures of working in a fast-paced entrepreneurial environment?*
I manage it quite well. In fact, I'd go so far as to say that I enjoy working in such an environment. The strategies that work for me consist of ensuring that I've got all the right skills to do the job, including good communications skills and the ability to work well with others. Just as important as skills, however, is the right state of mind. I enjoy working

at a fast pace and in a challenging environment where change is the only constant. I could not imagine myself working in a slow-paced and predictable environment.

Remember, the four steps simply provide a means by which you can capture lots of relevant data in a simple way. There's no reason why you cannot alter some aspects of the model to suit your own needs. It is designed to be flexible. Here are two important examples of how the four steps can be used differently.

First, you do not have to fill each column. For example, if you have no personal outcomes worth mentioning, don't invent them for the sake of filling out that section. The same goes for the obstacles under step 2. In some cases, people encounter very minor obstacles when performing certain duties—so minor, in fact, that they're really not worth mentioning. Always leave out trivia. The idea is to fill each of the columns only with information that was important to the job and that you think will be relevant to the interviewer.

Second, you can alter the headings under the four steps to suit the question you're addressing. For example, for questions that relate to qualities or issues that are not skills related and/or do not readily lend themselves to step-by-step procedures, the heading of the second column can be adjusted to simply read 'Examples'. Such qualities would include loyalty, honesty, integrity, work-related values or beliefs, and hobbies. Because values-related characteristics such as the above are qualities which do not require skills or technical knowledge, and which do not lend themselves to a sequence of actions, this column would simply list examples of when you behaved loyally or honestly (rather than how you did something). Here are some examples of questions where step 2 may be adjusted:

- Tell us about some of your interests outside of work.
- We're loyal to our employees and would like to think they are loyal to us. Can you give us an example of you behaving in a loyal manner?
- Do you prefer a quiet workplace or one in which there is some noise?

- Do you enjoy following rules?
- Do you prefer following established step-by-step procedures or making it up as you go?

Suggested activity: Using the four steps

- Select a duty or a job requirement that you're familiar with and, using the four steps to interview success, capture all the relevant information you can think of (see Table 3.1).
- When you've entered all your information, pose yourself two questions using the behavioural questioning technique referred to in this chapter.
- Practise your answers *aloud* until you've reached a satisfactory level of fluency.

Summary of key points

- 'Can you do the job?' questions are generally the most common questions asked at interviews. They are concerned with ascertaining your skills, knowledge and experience.
- 'Can you do the job?' questions can be split into three categories:
  - questions about duties that you have performed before;
  - questions about duties that you have not performed but whose skills you have mastered;
  - questions about duties that are entirely new to you.
- Your first important step to preparing your interview answers is to find out as much about the job as possible.
- The four steps to interview success provide a simple-to-use framework with which you can capture all the relevant information you need to construct interview answers. As well as capturing what you did and how you did it, it also compels you to think about context and outcomes. It is ideally suited for answering behavioural questions and can be used in a flexible way.

- Beware of long-winded answers.
- The most effective way of putting together the information you capture using the four steps is to pose to yourself hypothetical interview questions and then answer them out loud until you become fluent.
- A good interview answer will generally contain the following points:
  - a context;
  - specific examples;
  - what you did and how you did it;
  - outcomes;
  - it will get directly to the point.

4 Same skills, different job

Too often, people fail to make the link between their existing skills and the skills required for the job they want. As a result, they either do not bother applying, or they apply with the view that they'll probably not get the position.

By the end of this chapter, as well as showing you how to prepare for this type of question, I hope to persuade the skeptic in you that skills are often a lot more transferable than you may realise. Once you've assimilated this idea and learnt how to prepare answers for duties that you have not performed before but whose skills you have mastered, a whole new universe of jobs suddenly becomes potentially available. What makes learning how to prepare for this type of question even more important is that, unless you're interviewing for a job which is almost identical to those you've done in the past, it is likely to be the most common question asked.

So let's pose a question: what do a furniture salesperson and an insurance call centre operator have in common? Using the four steps to interview success, we can discover which skills are both available and transferable. Before we start the process, however, we need to work out what the overlapping skills are. In other words, we need to link the skills and knowledge sets for what you've already done and the job you're now applying for.

Let's say, for example, you've been working in an insurance call centre where your only contact with customers has been over the telephone and you wish to apply for a job as a face-to-face salesperson selling furniture—two seemingly very different jobs. You will, amongst other things, need to demonstrate how your call centre customer service skills are relevant to the new job's customer service requirements. An effective way of doing this is to work backwards, by making a list of the customer service skills required by a face-to-face furniture salesperson, then thinking of all the customer service skills in call centre work that are the same or similar. Table 4.1 shows how it can be done.

Table 4.1 Applying skills from one job to another

Customer service skills for furniture salesperson	Customer service skills for insurance call centre
Greeting customers using appropriate language, including body language	Greeting customers with correct verbal language including tone of voice
Inquiring about customers' needs by posing open-ended questions	Inquiring about customers' needs by asking questions and listening carefully
Having a thorough knowledge of furniture products on offer and trying to match these to the customer's needs	Having a thorough knowledge of insurance products on offer and trying to match these to the customer's needs
Knowing how to close a sale	Knowing how to close a sale
Being courteous and polite to customers who decide not to buy	Being courteous and polite to customers who decide not to buy

As you can see, even though insurance call centre operators and face-to-face furniture salespeople work in very different environments, there is a great deal of *overlap* in the skills required for both jobs. In the above example, the only real skills difference is the fact that call centre operators don't have to think about their body language. The big difference, of course, lies with product *knowledge*. So, in preparation for the upcoming furniture sales interview, I'd be rehearsing all the similarities between the two jobs and thinking of the best way to overcome the one obvious weakness—limited product knowledge.

The next time you think it's pointless applying for a job because the duties are seemingly very different, you might want to try the linking skills and knowledge set exercise before finalizing your decision.

Using the four steps

Once you've worked out the skills common to the two jobs, you can include the relevant skills under step 2. All you have to do is transfer the information in the second column of Table 4.1 to the step 2 column in Table 4.2 opposite. Remember, Table 4.2 is being filled out by an insurance call centre operator who wants to apply for a sales position in a furniture store.

Step 3: Context

Your next step is to fill in the third, or context, column of Table 4.2 opposite. However, talking about working in a call centre when you are applying for a job in a furniture store—notwithstanding the similar skills—is only going to highlight the *differences* between your past context and the job you're applying for. In this situation, you need to acknowledge your past job, but as briefly as possible. *Your job at the interview is to focus on the similarities between the two jobs, not the differences.* For this reason, there's hardly anything written in the context column.

Step 4: Outcomes

Unlike the context column, the outcomes column can contain a great deal of information. See Table 4.2 opposite for what might be included.

Putting it all together

Let's look at a sample question and answer that might occur in an interview for a new job with similar skills.

Table 4.2 The four steps applied to a different job with similar skills

Step 1	Step 2	Step 3	Step 4
Duties/ requirements of position that I'm applying for	What I've already done that relates directly to the duties listed under step 1, including overcoming obstacles	Current or past context	Outcomes— organisational and personal
Selling furniture in a furniture store	• Greeting customer with correct language, including correct tone of voice • Inquiring about customers' needs by asking questions and listening carefully. • Having a thorough knowledge of insurance products on offer and trying to match these to the customer's needs • Knowing how to close a sale. • Being courteous and polite to customers who decide not to buy	Working in a call centre	**Organisational** • Consistently achieved my sales targets and regularly exceeded them • Commended on levels of service by my supervisor • Never had a customer complain about me **Personal** • Demonstrated an ability to quickly learn about the products I was selling

Question: *Look, I like how you've presented yourself, but the fact that you've never worked in a furniture environment worries me.*
I can see your point. I think if I were in your shoes I'd be thinking the same thing. In my defence, I'd like to emphasise that I am able to bring to this job all the skills that you require. That's because call centre customer service skills are directly relevant to your business. For example, I am very experienced at greeting customers using correct language and tone of voice; I've mastered the skill of ascertaining customers'

needs by asking the right questions; and I understand the importance of quickly learning the ins and outs of all the products I am selling and linking this knowledge to the what the customer wants. I've also learned how to close a sale and I am acutely aware of the importance of being very polite to customers who decide not to buy because there's always the chance they might come back (step 2: skills).

My former employers consistently commended me on my customer service skills. I never received any negative feedback from customers and I always reached my targets and periodically exceeded them (step 4: organisational outcomes).

Also, I've demonstrated in all my past jobs an ability to learn about my products very quickly, so my limited knowledge about furniture will not be a problem. The fact is, I know a lot about furniture already. Furthermore, the reason I'm applying for this job is because I love furniture and home decorating. I'd like nothing more than to be able to work in such an environment (step 4: personal outcomes).

This answer has several very positive aspects:

- The initial response was not to disagree with the interviewer's reservation. The interviewee acknowledged the interviewer's hesitation by saying, 'I can see your point . . .' Acknowledging first and *then* putting your points forward is a much more effective technique than just disagreeing from the outset.
- Without delivering a long-winded dissertation on customer service skills, the applicant addressed the interviewer's reservations by succinctly linking all their existing customer service skills to the job.
- The interviewee kept talk about working in an insurance call centre to an absolute minimum.
- The interviewee highlighted the effectiveness of their customer skills by mentioning three positive outcomes.
- And finally, but very importantly, the applicant told the interviewer that they loved furniture and would like nothing more than to work in a furniture environment. There are few things

in life that employers like hearing more than potential employees saying they love the industry.

Suggested activity: Applying for a new job requiring similar skills

Write down the main skills and knowledge inherent in a job (preferably one you'd like to apply for) that's different to what you've been doing. Beside them, list all the similar skills and knowledge you have.

There are a number of skills that are common to many jobs. Some are fairly specific (e.g. being a good listener), whilst others are quite broad (e.g. good manager, team player). Note that many of these skills also overlap—for example, an effective team player needs to be a clear communicator and a good listener. On the whole, it's best to be as specific as possible.

Skills that are common to most jobs include:

- being a clear communicator;
- being a good listener;
- being an effective team player;
- willingness to help colleagues;
- being an effective planner;
- being a skilful organiser;
- the ability to work in a pressured environment;
- good customer service skills;
- the ability to close a sale;
- being good at dealing with angry customers;
- the ability to adapt to changing circumstances;
- being a good manager of people;
- managing time effectively;
- effective presentation skills;
- good analytical skills;
- the ability to motivate staff;
- being able to facilitate group discussions and meetings;

- being an effective negotiator;
- being a good on-the-job coach of staff;
- being a successful networker.

Suggested activity: Using the four steps

Once you've compared the two sets of skills, you may like to use the four steps to capture the information you need. Then ask yourself two or three behavioural-based questions and try answering them aloud until you're happy with the result.

Summary of key points

- Many people fail to appreciate the portability of their skills and knowledge. When they're looking for a new job, they only look at the job title or duties, not the skills underpinning those duties. Understanding that skills and knowledge can be portable between jobs can open up a whole new world of career opportunities.
- Before you discount a job that interests you, list the major skills and knowledge of that job and then beside that list your existing skills and knowledge. If there are a lot of matches, then go for it!
- Use the four steps to help prepare your answers.

5 Your potential to tackle **new** tasks

At times, you'll be asked questions that have nothing to do with your past duties and achievements. To make matters worse, the skills inherent in these duties will be substantially different to the skills you already have, thus making these the most challenging of all interview questions. Typically, you are asked these type of questions when you are starting off in your career, changing careers or going for a promotion that entails brand new duties such as managing a team of people. Clearly, when you have not performed the duties before, making a direct link to past duties or skills becomes problematic. However, there's no reason for despair. There are plenty of interviewees who successfully tackle these sorts of questions on a regular basis. As you have already learned, the key to success is correct preparation.

Break down the duties

The first step involves taking each of the new duties and *breaking them down into the individual skills and knowledge they comprise*. The individual pieces of information you come up with will constitute the core of your answers. In terms of our four steps, this information will go under step 2.

Breaking down a duty that you've never performed before can sometimes be a tricky exercise, particularly if you've had no experience in doing it. But don't give up—after a couple of tries it becomes easy. Here are some guidelines that you should find useful.

Begin by asking yourself the question, 'In order to perform a particular duty or requirement, what steps would I need to take?'

Conduct a brainstorming session. Do not overlook any detail, no matter how trivial you may think it is. Write down everything and anything that comes into your head. You can throw out the unimportant stuff later.

What may strike you as being trivial and not worth mentioning often turns out to be an important skill. A good example of this is listening skills. Most people don't even think about mentioning this skill, yet good listening skills are critical to effective interpersonal skills—including being a team player, problem-solving and conflict resolution. It's also a very hard skill to master, especially when you're hearing something that you don't agree with.

If you're having problems coming up with ideas, don't worry. Contact a friend, a work colleague, a former manager or anyone you think may be able to shed some light on the matter. You'll soon find that two or three heads are better than one. Whatever you do, don't give up. You *will* do it—it's just a matter of getting the hang of it.

If your friends can't help, don't panic. It's time to consult a book or an expert in the field. If, for example, you're applying for a manager's position and you've never managed people before, it makes sense to talk to someone who knows what's involved.

As much as possible try to list the component skills in a logical, sequential order.

Before you finalise your list, you must scrutinise your answers. Because you've never performed these duties before, it stands to reason that some of your answers may be somewhat naïve or just plain wrong. Scrutinise the quality of your answers by talking to someone who knows and/or by asking yourself the all-important question, 'Can I credibly support my answer if questioned in more detail by the interviewer?'

In most circumstances, there are no absolutely right or wrong answers to how duties are performed. Questions requiring highly technical answers which need to be very specific are, of course, the exception. As unique individuals working in varied environments, we face differing challenges which affect the way we do things. So the way I work in an entrepreneurial environment, or plan and organise my work, may be different to someone else's method—but it is no less valid or effective. In terms of interviews, the important thing is to provide a succinct and logical answer that can withstand scrutiny if the interviewer decides to delve deeper into your answer. And good interviewers *always* dig deeper.

You need to have faith in what you think is the right way to perform a duty, but be sure you have thought your answer through. Ask yourself, 'Why would I take a particular course of action?' By all means consult experts and listen carefully to what they say, but at the end of the day it has to be *your* answer.

Let's look at a common example of a new duty: managing people in the workplace. Managing staff, as anyone who has been thrust into that position knows, requires a range of new skills—some of which can be quite challenging. Given the importance most organisations place on effective people management, how you respond to this type of question could easily make or break your interview. Here are a few examples of managing staff questions:

- How would you go about leading a team of highly trained professionals?
- As a manager of people, how would you go about motivating them and maximising their performance?
- Describe your ideal manager.

Duties inherent in managing people in the workplace might include:

- delegating work appropriately, taking into account the abilities of staff and multi-skilling considerations;
- giving timely and objective feedback;
- consulting on matters that affect staff;
- acknowledging and recognising their efforts;
- treating everyone equally.

Using the four steps, you would include these duties—or others you might regard as important—under step 2 (see Table 5.1 opposite).

Create a relevant context

Given that you've never performed this duty, it stands to reason that you cannot provide a real-life context as you would for the duties you had actually performed. However, this should not prevent you from making up a context—one that will be the same or similar to the job you're applying for. Doing this compels you to go a step further by placing your step 2 answers in a 'real life' situation. By doing this, you'll be in a better position to make your answers sound more convincing.

In an interview, you are likely to be asked a contextualised question—that is, one which asks how you would perform a duty within a certain situation or context. So, instead of being asked 'How would you go about managing staff?' (no context), it is likely you'll have to answer a question more like 'How would you go about managing a team of highly motivated professionals in a fast-paced environment?'

If you do happen to be asked a question without a context (inexperienced interviewers have been known to ask decontextualised questions), being able to put it into a context that is relevant to the job you're applying for is likely to impress the interviewer. Without context, your answers will sound only half-completed.

Place your imaginary context under step 3 in the four steps to interview success table (see Table 5.1 opposite).

Expected outcomes

Given that you've never performed this duty before, it's nonsensical to talk about real outcomes. However, it is a good idea to think in terms of expected outcomes—that is, what is likely to happen if you manage people effectively. The advantages of thinking about expected outcomes are twofold. First, because outcomes are similar to goals, it will demonstrate to the interviewer that you're thinking in terms of goals or final results rather than just process. Remember, it is achieving goals that matters most to employers. Second, many interviewers are fond of asking annoying questions like, 'And what do you see the results of your people management approach being?' and, 'What can a good manager of people achieve with his/her staff?' Filling out the step 4 column with your expected outcomes will help you to formulate effective answers to such questions (see Table 5.1 below).

Be aware that some companies prefer not to use the term 'managing' people. Instead they favour the term 'leading' people. If you're preparing answers to a set of managing/leading people questions, make sure you acquaint yourself with the company's management language. Sometimes, just using the right word can make a big difference.

Table 5.1 Your potential to tackle new tasks

Step 1	Step 2	Step 3	Step 4
Duties/ requirements of position	What would I do to ensure the duties listed under step 1 are performed properly, including overcoming obstacles	Imaginary context	Expected outcomes— organisational and personal
Managing people in the workplace	• Delegating work appropriately, taking into account abilities of staff and multi-skilling considerations • Giving timely and objective feedback • Consulting on matters that affect staff • Acknowledging and recognising their efforts	Managing a small team of highly motivated professionals in a fast-paced environment	Organisational • Maintain or improve motivation of staff, which will contribute to improved individual and team performance, including possible improvement in rates of absenteeism and turnover Personal • Demonstrated an ability to quickly learn about the products I was selling

Putting it all together

Let's take a look at a likely question and a possible response.

Question: *How would you go about leading a team of highly trained professionals?*

I would certainly take into account the fact that I am dealing with professionals—that is, highly trained people who should know what they're doing (step 3). In delegating work, I would take into account their abilities, preferences and current workloads. I would make sure that work was distributed evenly, taking organisational needs into account (step 2).

I'm a great believer in giving people feedback. Without feedback staff often are unaware of important matters relating to their performance. I would ensure that my feedback was timely and objective—that is, based on facts rather than conjecture (step 2).

I also believe in consulting with staff in matters relating to their work. Not only do staff feel more valued when they're consulted, but often management can be made aware of important matters that they previously were not aware of (step 2).

Acknowledging and recognising individual and team effort is, I think, also very important—especially when it comes to giving staff a feeling of being appreciated. I know that when my manager acknowledged something special that I did, I always felt good about it (step 2).

I strongly believe that effective people management is vital to the success of any team. Good managers are able to motivate and bring out the best in their people. This in turn contributes significantly to the performance of the team. It would be my objective to maximise the performance of my team by implementing the techniques already mentioned (step 4).

The strengths of the above answer are as follows:

- acknowledging the professional context of the team to be managed;
- articulating the points in a clear and sequential order;
- giving reasons why certain actions would be taken;
- finishing off with an expected outcome.

Suggested activity: Your potential to tackle new tasks

To help you prepare your answers to at least one duty which is substantially different to anything you've done before, follow the guidelines described above—that is:

- Break the duty down into its individual components.
- Use the four steps and put those individual components under step 2.
- Use an imaginary context that is likely to come up in an interview.
- Include expected outcomes.

Summary of key points

- Questions about duties which are substantially different to anything you've done before are generally the most challenging in an interview.
- There is often no one single answer (nor one right answer) about how duties are performed. We all come from different work backgrounds and bring with us different ways of doing things.
- The names of steps 2, 3 and 4 will change slightly, reflecting the different challenges posed by these sorts of questions. In particular, the context (imaginary context) and outcomes (expected outcomes) headings change to take into account the fact that you've never performed these duties before.

6 'Are you the sort of **person** we can work with?'

Deciding you are someone an employer can work with is often what distinguishes the winning candidate in the mind of the interviewer, even though the interviewer may not consciously have asked questions to elicit such information.

'Are you the sort of person we can work with?' questions are designed to explore what you might be like to work with, including your attitudes about work. These could include your values, likes and dislikes, and general predispositions. One reason why these issues are important is because organisations, over a period of time, develop their own culture or way of interrelating and doing things. Some organisational cultures, for example, are predominately entrepreneurial—that is, dynamic, with one eye always on making a sale—whereas others may emphasise order, attention to detail and proper procedure. Cultures are largely determined by the nature of the business, as well as the personality and beliefs of senior management. Large organisations often have diverse subcultures coexisting (or trying to coexist).

In many interviews, there is really very little separating the talents of the job candidates. When employers are faced with equally good skills and experience, they will look at other factors to reach a decision. Arguably, the most important of these other factors is the likeability of the candidate. In tight labour markets, employers are usually inundated with candidates whose skills and experience exceed their needs. With such an embarrassment of riches the 'Are you the sort of person we can work with?' question assumes even greater importance.

It would be misleading to think that 'Are you the sort of person we can work with?' questions assume importance only when an interviewee has responded satisfactorily to the 'Can you do the job?' questions. More and more companies are realising that hiring people who have the technical know-how but cannot fit into the culture of their organisation can actually be bad for business. In the final analysis, a business consists of a group of people working together to achieve certain goals. If these people cannot get on with each other, or there are individuals who find it difficult to deal with the prevailing group dynamics, then there's a good chance the business will suffer in some way. In fact, some companies actually give greater weight to cultural fit issues than the skills and knowledge of the job candidates. Typically, these companies are the ones whose procedures and operating systems have been developed in-house and who therefore need to train people from the beginning to get them up to speed. For these sorts of companies, whether a candidate can actually do the job may not even be on the agenda.

How do I recognise an 'Are you the sort of person we can work with?' question?

Generally speaking, such questions are *indirect* in nature. Instead of being asked 'Are you the sort of person we can work with?' you are likely to be asked questions designed to understand how you work with other people in a variety of contexts. Here are some examples:

- Do you prefer working in a team environment or solo? Why?
- What makes you an effective team player?
- Describe your favourite manager's management style.
- Can you give us a specific example of working under pressure? What was the situation and how did you handle it? If you could do it again, how would you do it differently?

- What do you do when you're not getting on with someone in your workplace?
- What do you do when you cannot get a word in at your meetings?
- How do you handle someone who is demonstrating aggressive behaviour and intimidating others at a meeting?
- Describe the last time you had a falling out with someone at work. What did you do?
- What would you do if someone in your team was not pulling their weight?
- Imagine you are a team leader. One of your staff has just made a significant error. What do you say to this person?
- Why do you want to work for us?
- An irate customer rings you and has a go at you for something you're not responsible for. How do you handle it?
- Describe yourself. What interests do you have?

What if the question isn't asked?

Sometimes employers fail to ask 'Are you the sort of person we can work with?' questions. Usually it's not because they don't want to know; it's simply that they lack experience in interviewing. This is particularly the case with small to medium enterprises which lack in-house recruitment experience.

But even if you're not asked these sorts of questions, this remains an important issue for the interviewer. You need to address these issues by looking for opportunities during the interview to refer to your suitability. If you find an opening, use it to your advantage. Let's look at an example of how we could do this.

The example in the list above which relates to dealing with an irate customer may seem to be a customer service question. However, it can also be seen as an 'Are you the sort of person we can work with?' question! The most effective way to answer this question if you feel the interviewer is not delving deeply enough is to tackle it as both a 'Can you do the job?' and an 'Are you the sort of person we can work with?' question. Don't wait to be asked specific 'Are you the sort of person we can work with?' questions. View almost every question as an opportunity to plant seeds in the mind of the interviewer.

Below you'll find two brief answers to the question about the irate customer referred to on page 58. The first one treats the question as purely a 'Can you do the job?' one, whereas the second also incorporates an 'Are you the sort of person we can work with?' answer (the difference is in the first paragraph of the second answer).

> **Question**: *An irate customer rings you and has a go at you for something you're not responsible for. How do you handle it?*
>
> Answer 1: addressing the question as purely a 'Can you do the job?' question.
>
> First, I wouldn't take the aggression from the customer as a personal attack on me, otherwise I might want to argue back—which would be a mistake. I would listen carefully, without interrupting, to find out the cause of the customer's anger. I might ask a few questions to clarify matters if I was still a bit unclear at the end. Once I knew exactly what the causes of the customer's anger were, I'd look into coming up with a realistic solution. I would then explain to the customer what the solution would be, apologise for inconveniencing them and ask them if I could help them with something else.
>
> Answer 2: Addressing the question as both a 'Can you do the job?' question and an 'Are you the sort of person we can worth?' question.
>
> Experience has taught me that when customers are angry, there's usually a good reason for it. In fact, every time I'm dealing with a frustrated customer I see it as an opportunity to improve our operations. I ask myself what I can do so this doesn't happen again. I'm highly motivated by turning around unhappy customers.
>
> So first, I wouldn't take the aggression from the customer as a personal attack on me, otherwise I might want to argue back—which would be a mistake. I would listen carefully,

without interrupting, to find out the cause of the customer's anger. I might ask a few questions to clarify matters if I was still a bit unclear at the end. Once I knew exactly what the causes were, I'd look into coming up with a realistic solution. I would then explain to the customer what the solution would be, apologise for inconveniencing them and ask them if I could help them with something else.

Whilst both answers address the question effectively, the second answer contains an added dimension insofar as it provides a brief but effective insight into the values/beliefs of the interviewee. By doing this, it indirectly addresses the 'Are you the sort of person we can work with?' question. Any employer would be keen to work with someone who is highly motivated by turning around unhappy customers.

There is no excuse not to address the 'Are you the sort of person we can work with?' question if you follow the above example. The reality is that most questions can be used as a vehicle to address this fundamental question. It's about being a pro-active interviewee as opposed to a passive one. Look for opportunities to put yourself in the best possible light rather than simply waiting for good questions.

If you are asked

So far we've looked at how to address the 'Are you the sort of person we can work with?' question when you're not directly asked. However, there will be plenty of times when you will have to address the question directly—particularly if you're sitting before an experienced interviewer. The key to giving a good answer lies, as always, with correct preparation. Here's what to do.

Work out what the employer is looking for

There are at least eight qualities that all employers desire in their employees. These are:

- loyalty;
- a good work ethic;
- flexibility and adaptability to changing circumstances;
- honesty;
- willingness to learn new things;
- cooperative behaviour (being a team player);
- ability to cope with pressure;
- initiative.

Whilst the above list is not exhaustive, there is a good chance that one or more of these eight universal qualities (named because of their widespread popularity amongst employers) will be the focus of at least one interview question.

As well as preparing answers dealing with the eight universal qualities, it is also a good idea to try to ascertain the dominant culture or business values of your prospective workplace. Some workplaces, for example, purposefully encourage a culture of 'we're one big happy family', whereas others might promote the values of discipline and a strict adherence to rules. Your job is to try to correctly ascertain what the dominant culture and values are, and prepare accordingly. The safest way of doing this is by talking to the person who is going to interview you. Here are some examples of approaches you can make:

- I've heard on the grapevine that your company is keen on promoting a culture of outstanding customer service.
- My research indicates that quality control is your number one priority.
- I understand that your company highly values a team approach to getting the job done.

Be careful here, however. Ascertaining organisational culture/values can be difficult and dangerous. Suffice to say that organisations, in particular the larger ones, have multiple subcultures coexisting and competing against each other, and these subcultures are generally in a state of flux. If the dominant culture/values are not glaringly obvious, it is better to avoid speculating and perhaps getting it wrong. The last thing you want to do is prepare the wrong answers. If in doubt, stick to the eight universal qualities.

Putting an answer together

Once you've decided what the employer is looking for, your next step is to put together a convincing answer. The good news is that a number of the eight universal qualities will overlap with your 'Can you do the job?' questions—for example, flexibility, cooperative behaviour, coping with pressure and a good work ethic.

Once you've prepared your answers to the 'Can you do the job?' questions, look at the eight universal qualities and see which ones you haven't covered. The four steps to interview success are helpful here. Let's use them to address the work ethic question.

Here's a standard work ethic question and a possible answer.

Question: *In this company we do not stand for people who are not committed to their work. We'd like to think that all of us give our best. Can you give us an example of a time you had to go the extra mile?*

I believe that it is important for everyone in a team to try their best. I've always given my best and I believe the high quality of my work is testimony to that.

When I worked for Hannibal Enterprises, for example, sales orders of elephants would not go through unless I transferred the correct information to our suppliers. On two occasions there was a mix up with the information which threatened the sales. To remedy the situation, I stayed back until midnight to ensure that the information was correct and the sales went through. Even though I was not responsible for the initial mistake and did not have to stay back, I did so because I felt it was the right thing to do.

On another occasion we brought in a new software system—The Carthaginian—which was quite complex and full of set-up glitches. Because there was no time to learn all of it on the job, I stayed back several nights after work, on

Table 6.1 Addressing the issue of a good work ethic using the four steps

Step 1	Step 2	Step 3	Step 4
Duties/ requirements of position	What I did to ensure the duties listed under step 1 were performed properly, including overcoming obstacles	Context	Outcomes— organisational and personal
A good work ethic	• When required, I always stayed back to complete the relevant tasks • On occasions, I stayed back for several hours; otherwise the sales might have fallen through • The introduction of new software required a great deal of new learning; because there was no time to learn all of it on the job, I stayed back on several evenings to ensure that I quickly got on top of it • I ensured that minor problems were addressed quickly because un-attended minor problems often become major headaches	Working for Hannibal Enterprises, I had to meet important deadlines regarding information relating to sales orders. Failure to meet those deadlines meant the loss of sales.	Organisational • There were no sales losses or dissatisfied customers whilst I was at the helm • I trained others in the use of the new software system

my own initiative, to ensure that I got on top of it—which I did. As a result of my efforts, I was able to train other people in its use, which saved us considerable time and money.

Remember that characteristics such as loyalty and honesty are not skills based, and do not readily lend themselves to step-by-step procedures. In these instances, all you need do is think of specific examples where you demonstrated loyalty and/or honesty. Try to think of examples relating to work; however, if you are not able to do this, non-work examples will suffice. Here are two such questions and possible answers.

Loyalty question: *We value employee loyalty highly. Do you regard yourself as a loyal person?*
I value loyalty a great deal. I'd like to think that I am a loyal friend and employee, and that those who are close to me are the same.

I've demonstrated loyalty on numerous occasions. In my previous job, for example, I was approached many times by employment consultants to see whether I was interested in working for other companies. Furthermore, many of these offers came with the promise of higher pay. On every occasion I declined these approaches because I felt a strong sense of loyalty to my employer, who had gone to considerable lengths and expense to train me as well as make me feel a valued member of the team. He placed a great deal of trust in me and in turn I felt I could trust him completely. My values are such that I would much prefer working in an environment where loyalty is a given and is extended by both parties.

Honesty question: *The work we do requires a great deal of honesty and trust. We trust our people to do the right thing without continually looking over their shoulders. Can you tell us about a time you demonstrated honesty?*
In all my jobs I've had to demonstrate honesty and I've never given an employer the slightest reason to doubt my integrity. In fact, I've always been trusted with handling large sums of money and highly sensitive information. For example, when I was working for the Wellington Project I was in charge of storing and transferring highly sensitive data. In fact, I was only one of three people who had access to the information which was critical to the survival of the company. Had this information been leaked there was a very real possibility that

our competitors, especially the French, would have captured the segment of the market that we relied upon most heavily.

Both the above answers address the issues of loyalty and honesty in a positive and persuasive manner. They do this by:

- starting off with a confident affirmation;
- going directly to the heart of the matter; then
- providing specific examples.

Suggested activity: The eight universal qualities

Try preparing your answers to each of the eight universal qualities using the four steps.

If you're about to attend an interview and you're certain of the culture of the workplace, you could prepare an answer addressing the requirements of that culture.

Summary of key points

- 'Are you the sort of person we can work with?' questions, although generally not as frequent as the 'Can you do the job?' questions, are just as important and in some cases even more so.
- Even if you're not asked 'Are you the sort of person we can work with?' questions, you should attempt to address the issue by looking for opportunities to talk about your relevant attributes.
- All employers are keen on hiring people who possess the following eight universal qualities (so preparing responses to these qualities makes a lot of sense):
  - loyalty;
  - a good work ethic;
  - flexibility and an ability to adapt to changing circumstances;
  - honesty;
  - willingness to learn new things;

     — cooperative behaviour (being a team player);
     — coping with pressure;
     — initiative.

- Where possible, try to ascertain the dominant culture or work values of the place you're applying to work in and prepare your answers accordingly. But make absolutely sure that a definite culture exists and your information is correct. Otherwise, just stick to eight universal qualities.

7 Employers love **motivated** employees

Experienced employers know that highly motivated employees are invaluable. Motivated employees tend to learn things quickly, complete their duties enthusiastically, care about the business and often go beyond the call of duty. Contrast this with an unmotivated employee. Even highly talented people who lack motivation can border on the ineffectual. As one successful employer said to me:

> Give me motivation over talent any day. Motivated people develop talent by their drive and enthusiasm. They ask questions, volunteer for jobs and overcome any shortcoming they may have. They're worth twice as much as talented people who lack motivation. An unmotivated talented person is an oxymoron.

Communicating your motivation levels

At interviews, the motivation levels of the candidate tend to be inferred by the interviewers. In other words, the interviewer picks up on signals given by the interviewee. These signals can be broken down into three groups:

- what is said;
- how it is said;
- body language.

This chapter will focus on the first two groups—what is said and how it is said. Chapter 9 will discuss body language. Suffice to say that convincing employers you're highly motivated rests on more than just the words that come out of your mouth. Your body language and the way you say things are both critical.

Despite the critical importance of motivation in the workplace, motivation questions are not as common as they should be. One reason for this is that there are many inexperienced interviewers out there who are not sure how to construct a motivation question. Questions such as, 'How motivated are you?' sound embarrassingly amateurish and tend to attract answers such as, 'I am very motivated. If you give me this job I'll work very hard.'

When direct motivation questions *are* asked, they usually begin with the words 'why' and 'what'. Here are some classic examples:

- Why do you want to work here?
- Why do you want to do this job?
- What interests you about this job?
- What are the things you like about working in this sort of environment?
- What do you love about this work?
- What are the sorts of things you enjoy doing at work?

A useful way to prepare for all of the above questions is to ask yourself 'What are the things that I like about this job?' Or, to put it another way, 'Why do I like this sort of work?'

When thinking about what you like about a particular job, you need to look at the duties of the job very carefully (see the section on job advertisements in Chapter 3). Your next step is to make a list of all the things that attract you to the job, being as specific as possible. You need to be specific, otherwise your answers may sound hollow. A broad-ranging statement such as 'I love retail', for example, is not nearly as convincing as 'I love interacting with people on a daily basis' or 'I love the thrill of making a sale and watching a happy customer leave the store'. That's because the last two statements not only tell the interviewer that you love retail, but also explain why.

Here are some examples of motivation statements that excite

employers (but make sure you've got the specific examples to back up your statement):

- I love working with people.
- I very much enjoy challenges of the sort you mention.
- I really like working with numbers.
- Interacting with people is what gets me out of bed in the mornings.
- I really enjoy working on my own.
- I love learning new things.
- I love selling.
- Solving complex problems is what I love doing most.
- I get a deep sense of satisfaction when I make a customer happy.
- I'm very keen on solving technical issues.
- I love working on computers.
- I really go for working in this sort of environment.
- I can't get enough of this kind of work.

Don't hide your enthusiasm

You will have noticed that all of the above statements have one very important quality in common: they're all enthusiastically expressed. Avoid timid or uncertain language because you will sound unconvincing. Put yourself in the shoes of an employer and compare the following two answers about customer service. Which of the two would you rather hear at an interview?

Answer 1: On the whole I like dealing with customers even though they can be really irritating and do ask stupid questions. But I do realise that without customers I'd be out of a job so I make a big effort to satisfy them.

Answer 2: I love dealing with customers. I really enjoy the interaction with people, including answering all their questions—no matter how trivial they may seem. I get a deep sense of satisfaction when I can solve problems for customers or help them out in some way.

Clearly, the second answer is the better one. It starts off with a very enthusiastic statement and reinforces this with several more affirmations. It is full of positive energy and gives the clear impression that the person is highly motivated in terms of providing high standards of customer service. Notice also that this answer makes a value statement—that is, 'I get a deep sense of satisfaction'. By doing so, it gives us an insight into the beliefs or values of the speaker and hence partly addresses the 'Are you the sort of person we can work with? question.

On the other hand, the first answer sounds as though the person provides good customer service because they're forced to. We all know that customers sometimes ask stupid questions, but interviews aren't the place to articulate such views.

The information you've gathered using the four steps can also be used to address motivation questions. The information under step 2 can be a rich source of specific information when addressing the motivation question. Let's say, for example, that you're applying for a job in which you have to lead a team of people and you're asked one of the classic motivation questions. Here's what the exchange might sound like:

Question: *What interests you about this job?*
There are many things that really interest me about this job. One of them is the opportunity to lead a team of hard-working people. I love bringing out the best in people and watching them get the most out of their work. **I am able to do this by applying sound principles of team leadership. For example, when delegating work, I take into account people's abilities as well as workload. I give timely and consistent feedback designed to improve people's performance. I consult with people, acknowledge good work and treat everyone equally.** Getting respect from your team is a highly motivating experience.

The bold section of the above answer is taken directly from the second column of Table 5.1. By stating specifically what you do to successfully lead a team of people, you're giving credibility to your claim about enjoying 'bringing out the best in people'.

The exciting thing about this answer is that it works on several levels:

- It answers the question directly.
- It tells the interviewer that you're probably a great team leader.
- It tells the interviewer that bringing out the best in people is something that motivates you a great deal.
- It does all of the above without waffling.

A word of warning about motivators

When compiling your answers about the things that you like about the job, there are some things that you need to be careful with. These include:

- money;
- proximity to where you live;
- convenient hours;
- friends working there.

All of these can be important motivators for many people—and can, of course, be mentioned during the course of the interview. However, they should not be mentioned as primary motivators *because none of them has anything to do with you performing well in the job*. Primary motivators should be linked to the nature of the work itself, and should demonstrate an ability to perform well in key areas of the job. It is much more effective to say that you love working with people rather than that you love the money or your travelling time will be halved!

Suggested activity: Motivation

Make a list of all the things that attract you to your chosen job. If you're having problems coming up with answers, take a close look at the main duties and ask yourself, 'What is it about these duties that I like?' Remember to avoid broad statements. Be as specific as you can. Once you've compiled your list, answer the following questions. Keep on practising your answers until you're happy with your fluency.

Question 1: Why have you applied for this job?
Question 2: What are the sorts of things that motivate you?

Summary of key points

- Convincing interviewers that you're highly motivated requires more than saying the right things. Body language and how you say things are just as important.
- When preparing your answers to motivation questions, one of the helpful questions you can ask yourself is 'Why do I like this kind of work?' Your specific responses to this question will constitute the core of your motivation answers.
- Express yourself with enthusiasm. Interviewers expect to see keenness in motivated candidates.
- Step 2 of the four steps is often a good source of information for motivation questions.
- Avoid mentioning motivators such as money and travel time—they do not contribute to your ability to perform well in the job.

8 The 'big five' questions

There are five very common generic questions which crop up in virtually every interview. They relate to:

- being a good team player;
- planning and organising your work effectively;
- good interpersonal communication;
- coping with change in the workplace;
- providing effective customer service (including internal customers).

Using the four steps, this chapter poses the questions about these issues and suggests possible responses.

The importance of the 'big five' questions

The skills listed above are *vital* to most jobs. It is hard to think of a job in which all five do not come into play at one stage or another, and impossible to think of a job in which at least one of them is not relevant. For this reason, the 'big five' actually constitute hundreds of interview questions.

Once you've learned how to answer the 'big five' questions, you will be able to respond to many other questions because there is a great deal of overlap amongst them. For example, if you can answer the basic question, 'What makes you a good team player?' you should also be able to respond to a range of similar team player questions, including:

- How do you like working in a team?
- Do you consider yourself a good team player?
- Describe your ideal team.
- What does it take to be an effective team player?

However, be aware that, while learning how to respond to one generic question allows you to answer many similar questions, this does not mean you will be able to answer every conceivable question asked. It's up to you to be diligent and look for questions within the genre that may be slightly different or unexpected.

Given the common nature of the above skills, they will be treated as if they have been performed before.

Answering a 'team player' question

Most people work in teams. Even people who appear to work on their own often have to interact with others in the organisation, thus creating one or more loosely formed teams. Some teams need to work closely together, others less so; some teams work together all the time, whereas others meet only periodically. The important point is that employers rely heavily on the smooth functioning of their teams and are keen to hire effective team players. Here are some examples of team player questions:

- What makes you a good team player?
- How do you find working in a team?
- Do you prefer working alone or in a team? Why?
- What do you dislike about working in a team?
- What would you do if one of your colleagues was not pulling their weight?
- Describe your ideal team.
- Can you give us examples of what you've done to ensure that your role in a team was a positive one?

- How would you handle a team member who was loud and aggressive at team meetings and dominated proceedings by intimidating others?

Now let's use the four steps to prepare the information needed to respond to 'team player' questions:

Table 8.1 Being an effective team player

Step 1	Step 2	Step 3	Step 4
Duties/ requirements of position	What I've done to ensure the duties listed under step 1 were performed properly, including overcoming obstacles	Context	Outcomes— organisational and personal
Effective team player	• Acknowledging others' opinions and contributions • Helping colleagues when they've run into obstacles • Sharing important information and know-how • Avoiding anti-social behaviours such as dominating team discussion or shouting colleagues down • Joining a team in which there were communication problems, I suggested a different meeting format which improved communications	Working in the payroll team, we were responsible for paying approximately 2000 employees	**Organisational** • Halved pay errors within two months of operations • Contributed to improved communication amongst team members **Personal** • Learned a great deal about working in payroll, including how to operate payroll software

Here's a sample interview question and a possible response.

Question: *Are you a good team player? Can you give us examples of you demonstrating team player capabilities?*
Yes, I consider myself to be an effective team player. In my previous job I was part of a team of four people who were responsible for paying the salaries, including overtime and bonuses, of approximately 2000 employees (step 3: context).

When I first started work in the team, there were communication problems between several team members. As well as affecting our performance, these problems were straining relations between certain members of the team. After several weeks, I thought that if we introduced more regular meetings and a rotating chair, communications might improve. When I made this suggestion, the team members agreed to it and, to make a long story short, the new meeting format turned out to be a success. Both communications and performance improved (step 2: overcoming an obstacle).

I also demonstrated my team player capabilities by making a point of acknowledging my colleagues' opinions and contributions, as well as helping team members when they were having problems. I think when you're willing to help others, they'll help you when you need it in return—and that can only be good for the team. I also made a point of sharing all information I thought my colleagues needed to know. I would mention even seemingly unimportant information such as individuals griping about their pay and minor mishaps with the software because often it can be the little things that cause big problems down the line (step 2: the what and how).

According to my colleagues, my presence in the team led to improved communications amongst team members, as well as with our clients, which contributed significantly to our overall performance. In particular, our error rate was halved within two months (step 4: outcomes).

Remember that, unless the interviewer has specifically told you that the company is placing a great deal of emphasis on hiring someone with effective team player skills, chances are that you would not use every aspect of the above answer in response to a single question. You may decide to use parts of it and keep the rest in reserve for a follow-up question or a question seeking information about similar skills. It is wise to over-prepare and even wiser to know when to stop. The same principle applies to the rest of the 'big five' questions.

Answering a planning and organising question

It is difficult to think of a job in which is no planning and organising are involved. If we accept that technology has largely taken over many of the repetitive tasks performed by people in the past, most jobs these days involve some sort of planning and organising. Planning and organising questions are therefore likely to be high on the agenda of many interviewers. Here are some typical planning and organising questions.

- Tell us how you go about planning and organising your work schedule.
- Can you give us an example of when you had to plan and organise an important event or work-related activity? What steps did you take?
- Do you consider yourself a good planner and organiser? Why?
- What do you do when your manager asks you to complete a task but you've already got a very full agenda?
- How do you prioritise your work?
- Describe your approach to planning and organising your work.

Table 8.2 shows how the four steps can help you prepare for this type of question.

Now let's look at a sample interview question and response.

Question: *Can you give us an example of when you had to plan and organise an important event or work related activity? What steps did you take?*

Table 8.2 Planning and organising

Step 1	Step 2	Step 3	Step 4
Duties/ requirements of position	What I did to ensure the duties listed under step 1 were performed properly, including over-coming obstacles	Context	Outcomes— organisational and personal
Planning and organising work	• Diarising work on a daily, weekly and/or monthly basis • Planning for contingencies • Keeping abreast of upcoming events and working out how they may affect my work • Prioritising my work according to the needs of the organisation • Never taking on more work than I can handle • Keeping communication channels with all stakeholders continually open	Working in the administration support unit for Michael Angelo Enterprises, which employed over 1000 people, I was working in a small team which was responsible for a broad range of duties ranging from ordering all painting supplies to security, building maintenance and assisting departments and managers with basic infrastructure needs.	**Organisational** • Our clients rated our service 'very high' for three years in a row **Personal** • I learned a great deal about what it takes to maintain an organisation in terms of infrastructure support

When I was working in the administration support unit for Michael Angelo Enterprises, I was responsible for planning a broad range of activities ranging from the timely ordering of paint supplies to security, building maintenance and assisting departments and managers with basic infrastructure needs (step 3: context).

Juggling all these activities simultaneously meant I had to plan my work in great detail as well as be very well organised.

There was one time when we had to install new security systems and new computer graphics software, as well as answering the multiple requests made by our clients. In order to deal with all of this, I needed to diarise my work on a daily, weekly and monthly basis and ensure that I continually kept up to date with what everyone else was doing. I made sure I attended as many meetings as I could and kept my ear to the ground. Given the multiple tasks I had to complete, I found it important to prioritise my work according to the needs of the organisation, as opposed to the needs of a few individuals. Getting the new security systems in place had to come before some of the requests made by managers. And, finally, it was important to learn how to say 'no' to some requests. In my view, a good planner knows how much is enough. Taking on more work than one can handle only leads to poor-quality service or even failure to do the work (step 2: the what and how).

As well as learning a great deal about what it takes to maintain an organisation in terms of infrastructure support, one of the great outcomes of my actions was that my clients rated my service as 'very high' for three years running, which gave me a great deal of satisfaction (step 4: outcomes).

Answering an interpersonal communication question

Interpersonal communication skills are not just about clear communications. They are also about the way we interact with others. People with effective interpersonal communication skills are much more likely to get on with others in the workplace (and thus get ahead) because they demonstrate a range of behaviours that bring out the best in the people they interact with. They are good listeners, avoid inflammatory language (including body language), acknowledge others' contributions, consult before making decisions, and so on.

People with effective interpersonal communication skills are highly prized by employers because they bring harmony to the workplace. They usually make people feel better about themselves and their contributions—which, of course, is important to employers in terms of maintaining a happy and productive workforce.

Here are some typical interpersonal communication skills questions:

- Do you enjoy working with people?
- How would you describe your relations with others in the workplace?
- Describe yourself. (Whilst this question does not confine itself to interpersonal communication skills, it does provide an excellent opportunity for you to briefly mention them.)
- Tell us about a time when you had a disagreement with someone at work. What were the circumstances and how did you deal with it?
- Can you give us an example of when you had to communicate a complex and sensitive issue? How did you go about it?
- Describe the colleague with whom you enjoyed working most.
- How do you deal with an angry person at work?
- Would you prefer to be seen as a well-liked person or an effective person?

A clear overlap exists between interpersonal communication skills and team player skills. Many of the points can therefore be used interchangeably.

Table 8.3 shows how the four steps can be used to prepare an answer to this type of question.

Here's an example of a possible interview question and response.

Question: *Can you give us an example of when you had to communicate a complex and sensitive issue? How did you go about it?*

When I was working for Magellan, I was on the team that was responsible for introducing a new performance appraisal system for all of the crew on our ship. Working on this project, I was often required to communicate complex and sensitive information to individuals and groups. I'd like to emphasise

Table 8.3 Interpersonal communication

Step 1	Step 2	Step 3	Step 4
Duties/ requirements of position	What I did to ensure the duties listed under step 1 were performed properly, including overcoming obstacles	Context	Outcomes— organisational and personal
Effective interpersonal communication skills	• Taking the time to listen to what others had to say, even if I didn't like what I was hearing • Communicating clearly, taking into account my audience and avoiding jargon • Using positive, non-threatening body language at all times • Acknowledging others' opinions and contributions • Consulting before making decisions	When I was working for Magellan, I was on the team that put together a performance appraisal system	Organisational • Contributed to the successful implementation of a performance appraisal system, with minimal resistance Personal • Gained much satisfaction from creating good working relationships with colleagues

that performance appraisals were an extremely sensitive issue because people's pay was being attached to the results (step 3: context).

I was successful in communicating the relevant information because I adhered to a number of sound interpersonal communication principles—principles that I have successfully implemented in the past. For example, I made a point of taking people's sensitivities into account and addressing them early on in our conversations. I avoided any form of jargon, and often assumed that my audience had very little prior knowledge about the issues at hand. I used positive, non-threatening body language—especially when I was confronted by the sceptics who belittled the program despite their lack of knowledge about it. I also acknowledged other people's opinions and never made disparaging comments about suggestions, no matter how outlandish they were (step 2: the what and how).

Furthermore, I always made the effort to consult with key stakeholders before finalising decisions. The very fact that you make the effort to consult and explain the parameters within which you have to work often minimises levels of dissatisfaction, even though people may not entirely agree with you.

As a result of my efforts, opposition to the program was virtually non-existent. The crew demonstrated a constructive attitude and gave it their best. As a result, we were able to successfully implement the program within our timeframe and budget.

Coping with change in the workplace

Unlike the workplace of yesteryear, when people could be performing the same set of duties for many years, today's work environment is characterised by constant change. In fact, it can be argued that the only constant is change. All this, of course, means a flexible employee is a highly valued one. Change can take the form of any number of things, including:

- new machinery;
- new procedures or guidelines;
- new legislation;
- new management structures;
- company takeovers;
- downsizing;
- new software;
- the effects of new competition.

Organisations that are unable to adapt quickly to changing circumstances often lose market share and can easily go out of business. Therefore, how you respond to 'coping with change' questions is very important. Here are a few examples of the form they may take:

- Tell us about a time you had to learn new things about your job. How did you cope?
- Do you enjoy changing duties?
- How do you cope with constant change in the workplace?
- Do you regard yourself as a flexible sort of person?

Table 8.4 Coping with change in the workplace

Step 1	Step 2	Step 3	Step 4
Duties/ requirements of position	What I did to ensure the duties listed under step 1 were performed properly, including overcoming obstacles	Context	Outcomes— organisational and personal
Coping with change in the workplace	• Understanding that change is the only constant in the modern workplace. Avoiding change often means falling behind. • I embraced retraining and new ways of doing things such as new software packages, new accounting methods, new legislation re safety procedures, etc • I think of change as the only way to keep my skills up to date, thus maintaining my employability	Whilst I was working for the Northern Legions, new technology was introduced, including machinery, software and procedures	Organisational • The new technology was successfully implemented within time and budget Personal • I learned a new and more efficient way of doing things

- How do you think you would react if you suddenly had to aban-don a project you were working on and start a new one?
- What are your views on learning in the workplace?

Table 8.4 shows how the four steps can be used to prepare answers for questions such as these.

Now let's look at a sample question and a possible response.

Question: *Tell us about a time you had to learn new things about your job. How did you cope?*

When I working for Northern Legions building Hadrian's Wall, senior management decided to invest heavily in new technology which was designed to improve quality and save us a great deal of time. This new technology involved an array of new equipment, software and work procedures, and represented a sea change in how I performed my duties (step 3: context).

Initially, all of us were slightly daunted at the grand scale of the changes; however, I soon realised that the changes were inevitable if our company was to remain competitive. I also quickly came to the realisation that, if I was to remain a valued member of the company, I would need to quickly learn how to work under the new regime. This realisation ensured that I embraced the changes enthusiastically. Whereas some of my colleagues saw it as a burden, I saw it as the way of the future—which is how I've come to view change generally. As well as attending all the required training sessions, I attended extra ones as well. I studied hard, asked questions and gained as much experience as I could. I soon became the acknowledged expert in certain areas, and people started coming to me for advice (step 2: the what and how).

As a result of our efforts, the new technology was successfully implemented. My team was working with the new technology within the timelines and budget allocated to us. And I learned a whole new way of doing things (step 4: outcomes).

Providing effective customer service (including internal customers)

One of the enduring myths in the workplace is the notion that customer service principles only apply to employees who deal directly with paying customers. Anybody else doesn't really count as a customer, and therefore doesn't have to be treated with the same care and sensitivity. This is a dangerous notion—one which frequently contributes to entrenched poor customer service (employees dealing directly with paying customers are often only as good as the support and service they receive from their colleagues in the back office).

In the final analysis, *every* job provides a form of customer service. It doesn't matter whether you're making the tea or negotiating a multi-million dollar deal. Highly effective companies practise high levels of customer service throughout the entire company. This is what some customer service questions may sound like:

- Tell us about a time you had to deal with a difficult customer. How did you deal with the situation and what was the outcome?
- Can you describe a time when you gave excellent levels of customer service? What did you do to make it so good?
- What does good customer service mean to you?
- What are the fundamentals of providing high levels of customer service?
- Do you think of yourself as a service-orientated person? Why?
- What importance do you attach to service? Why?

Table 8.5 shows how the four steps can be used to prepare responses to customer service questions.

Here's a sample question and possible response dealing with customer service.

Question: *Can you give us a recent example of when you had to provide good customer service? How did you go about it?*
A recent example of being required to give consistently high levels of customer service was when I was working in the accounts section of Guillotin. My duties involved dealing

Table 8.5 Providing effective customer service

Step 1	Step 2	Step 3	Step 4
Duties/ requirements of position	What I did to ensure the duties listed under step 1 were performed properly, including internal customers	Context	Outcomes— organisational and personal
Coping with change in the workplace	• I always listened to what the customer had to say and never made assumptions about the customer's needs • I gained an in-depth understanding of the products and services • By listening carefully and asking the right questions, I was able to match our product or service to the customer • I never over-promised • I understood that, without customers, I would have no job	Working in an accounts receivable/payable environment for Guillotin, in which monthly and annual reports had to be submitted. These duties required dealing with both internal and external clients.	Organisational • All customers received consistently good levels of customer service, including the implementation of service-level agreements Personal • Satisfaction of a job well done and receiving great feedback

with both internal customers—that is, the various departmental managers—as well as external customers, including people who owed us money and accounts that we needed to pay (step 2: context).

The steps I took to ensure that I was providing consistently good customer service were often the same for both the internal and external customers. Experience has taught me that customer service principles are universal. A good example of this was when I was dealing with our departmental managers. I never made the mistake of assuming I knew what they needed from me, even though we had worked together for several years. Things change and one has to keep up with those changes in order to provide good levels of service. At our meetings, I always made the point of finding out what all our managers were doing and what their upcoming projects were. If I knew something was coming up, I could plan for it and thus ensure good service. I also made sure that I had a detailed understanding of all our new services and products, and how these could benefit all our customers. For example, the acquisition of a new database allowed me to provide managers with much more up-to-date detail about our customers (step 3: the what and how).

As a result of this process, we were able to draw up a set of service delivery agreements with the various managers which gave us relevant guidelines and customer service targets. These service delivery targets played an important role in terms of our section receiving consistently positive feedback from our managers and avoiding redundancy (step 4: outcomes).

Suggested activity: The 'big five' questions

Try using the four steps to address the 'big five' questions using *your own material*. Once you've filled in the four columns, answer several questions based on each of the 'big five'.

Summary of key points

- The importance of the big five questions is that they are based on skills required for most, if not all, jobs. This makes it highly likely that you will be required to answer a number of questions relating to these. As well as the universality of these skills, they are also critically important to most employers (good interpersonal communication skills, for example, are seen as central to establishing harmonious work relationships and effective performance).

- How you answer a question relating to any one of the big five could make or break your interview.
- By using the recommended four steps you will be able to easily create your own answers to a wide range of questions relating to the following five skills: being a good team player; planning and organising your work effectively; having good interpersonal communication; coping with change in the workplace; and providing effective customer service (including internal customers).

9 Building **rapport** and trust

There are several things you can do to improve rapport-building and the development of trust during the course of the interview. As already mentioned, successful interviewees do more than just answer questions correctly. They also convince interviewers that they are the sort of people the interviewer can work with. Of course, answering questions in a convincing manner goes a long way towards establishing rapport and trust; however, there's a lot more to it than simply articulating a series of technically correct responses.

Stated in its simplest terms, building rapport and trust (R&T) during an interview requires that you *show the interviewer that you're a good person to work with by demonstrating the appropriate behaviours during the interview*. For example, it is self-defeating to tell the interviewer that you're a great team player but sit throughout the interview looking as though you could frighten paint off the wall. In short, you need to back up your words with your actions.

Managing perceptions and preconceived views

Interviews are largely about managing the perceptions of the interviewer. Studies show that people look for things that they believe (perceive) will be there, and conversely ignore—or pay less attention to—those things that don't fit into their preconceived views. If interviewers think that you are an outstanding prospect, there's a good chance that they'll be looking for, and registering, all the things that will support their preconceived notion. In other words, if two interviewees perform roughly the same at an interview, the interviewee with the better reputation prior to the interview will most likely be rated higher.

So, as much as possible, make the best impression you can before or at the very start of the interview. You can do this by:

- ensuring that your resume is the best that it can be;
- sending a positive and very brief pre-interview letter thanking the interviewer for the opportunity to be interviewed and stating how much you're looking forward to meeting them;
- contacting the company to make sensible pre-interview inquiries (see Chapter 3). Contacting the company before the interview demonstrates appropriate interest and a professional level of preparation.

First impressions

In addition, it is important to note that the first few minutes (some say seconds) of an interview are also very important in swaying the interviewer's mind. As the old adage goes, first impressions tend to be lasting impressions. Briefly (we'll cover these in more detail later on), the things to look for include:

- dress;
- handshake;
- eye contact;
- facial expressions;
- tone of voice.

Last impressions

People tend to recall more of what happens at the beginning and the end of an event than they do of what occurs in the middle. This does not mean you concentrate on the beginning and end of your interview and neglect the middle, however. It is a reminder to be careful about what you do and say towards the end. Some interviewees fall into the trap of over-relaxing (usually as a result of over-compensating for their initial tension) and straying into inappropriate behaviours such as becoming overly familiar and adopting an 'I'm at a barbecue' style of body language. So make sure you maintain appropriate interview behaviours right to the very end.

Communication is more than just words

One of the most important lessons you can learn about improving your rapport and trust ability is that there's much more to communication than the words that come out of your mouth. Communications experts constantly remind us that about 10 per cent of communication is represented by *what* we say, 30 per cent by *how* we say things and 60 per cent by our *body language!* So if, in your preparation for an interview you've been spending all your time concentrating on the content of your answers, you have effectively been spending 100 per cent of your efforts on 10 per cent of overall communication. This may go a long way towards explaining why so many people who give technically brilliant answers don't get the job.

Admittedly many interviewees understand intuitively that successful interpersonal communication (face-to-face communication) relies on much more than just the words used. However, for reasons too varied and complex to discuss here, there are many people whose interpersonal communication skills are not as well honed and/or who are unable to demonstrate their otherwise effective communication skills during an interview—probably because of heightened anxiety.

Once you understand that successful communication relies on a whole range of factors other than words, an entirely new world of communication begins to emerge. The focus of your interview preparations should shift from strict word preparation to include a whole range of non-verbals including such things as appearance, the way you sit and even when you nod your head. Sometimes a friendly smile and an acknowledging nod can be worth a lot more than the best verbal answers.

Modelling

An effective way of improving your interpersonal communication skills is by reading what the experts say and modelling those who you know are good at it. People you know who are genuinely popular usually possess highly developed interpersonal communication skills, even though they may not be aware of it. Next time you're with them, take a few minutes to observe all those little things they do and see what you can learn.

Modelling should be used as a guide only, however. Avoid over-mimicking or cloning someone else's behaviours. It is worth remembering that we are all different and what may work well for one person may not work for another. Learn to be selective and adopt only those things that you feel confident about.

Acknowledging the power source

In most interviews, there is an important yet unspoken dynamic lurking just beneath the surface. This dynamic is as old as the first time humans eyeballed each other and opened their mouths to grunt. Naturally, I'm talking about power. More specifically, I'm talking about acknowledging the fact that, in the vast majority of cases, the interviewer has the real power. (The exception to this is when you are lucky enough to possess a unique set of skills and/or knowledge that the employer is desperate to have.) If you are serious about maximising your rapport, it's important to demonstrate to the interviewer that you understand they have all the power when it comes to giving you the job.

As an interviewee, you too have power—primarily through the fact that you control what the interviewer will hear. However, this does not eliminate the reality that the power to hire (or not) lies exclusively with the interviewer. Interviewees who acknowledge the interviewer's power stand a better chance of being liked (and therefore winning the job) because, to put it bluntly, most human beings have a weakness for feeling important and having their egos stroked. Intuitively, many of us understand this dynamic but not everyone proactively demonstrates it during the interview. An interviewer may not even be aware of this dynamic (you can usually pick the ones who enjoy their power), but this doesn't mean it's not there.

Avoid grovelling

Acknowledging the power dynamics inherent in most interviews does not mean grovelling. As already mentioned, throwing yourself at the feet of the interviewer or laughing yourself hoarse at a lame joke will more than likely be seen as a form of deceit. The lesson here is a simple one: be aware of the underlying power dynamics present at most interviews and avoid behaviours (such as arguing a point or openly disagreeing with the interviewer) that will more than likely put the interviewer off.

Body language issues

Sitting

The way you sit communicates a great deal about a whole range of issues, including how important you think the interview is, how nervous (or confident) you are, and your understanding of the underlying power relations. Some people's sitting position exudes over-familiarity and even arrogance, whereas others communicate a serious lack of self-belief.

The golden rules in sitting are: avoid anything that will *distract* the interviewer from concentrating upon the content of your answers; and avoid making the interviewer feel *uncomfortable*. Interviewers generally do not feel comfortable if you sit in an aggressive way (leaning forward too much) or in an overly passive way (leaning back and crossing your legs at the thighs). In short, good sitting goes unnoticed by the interviewer. Here are some tips on what you should avoid:

- *Leaning back.* Gives the impression that you're not taking the interview seriously.
- *Crossing your legs at the thighs.* Too familiar, especially at the beginning of an interview.
- *Sitting with your legs wide apart.* Far too familiar for an interview situation, and can be both distracting and uncomfortable for the interviewer.
- *Leaning forward too much.* May make some interviewers feel uncomfortable, especially if you're physically big and talk loudly.
- *Slouching.* Gives the impression that you're not taking the interview seriously and will likely slouch in your duties.

Tips on good sitting practice include:

- *Straight and upright body.* This is a neutral sitting position that interviewers expect to see.
- *Male legs.* Males can keep their upper legs facing straight forward and adopt what is commonly referred to as the starters position—that is, the dominant foot flat on the ground with the other foot having only the front part touching the ground.
- *Female legs.* Females can cross their legs at the ankles and position the legs slightly to one side.

Facial expressions and eye contact

Facial expressions are extremely powerful communicators. If you're sitting correctly, the interviewer should spend most of the interview looking at your face and eyes. The two golden rules of sitting also apply here: do not do anything that will distract interviewers or make them feel uncomfortable. Anything that is *overdone* will almost certainly give the interviewer pause for concern, whether it be too much smiling, nodding or eye contact.

During the course of an interview, it is very important to control your facial expressions, especially if you feel the interview is not progressing to your satisfaction or you're hearing something you don't like—otherwise you may be communicating unwanted information to the interviewer.

Failure to control your facial expressions will undermine your credibility by sending conflicting signals to the interviewer. For example, say the interviewer suddenly tells you that the job will include a new and important duty that was not mentioned in the job ad and your immediate gut feeling reaction is, 'Oh no I didn't prepare for this new duty, and what the hell are they doing changing the job at this late stage and I know nothing about this new bloody duty!' But you say (or try to say), 'New duty, that's fine. I'm used to taking on new duties. I'm a fast learner and enjoy the challenge.' In this situation there's a good chance that the terror registered on your face will undermine your words and leave the interviewer unconvinced despite a reasonable answer.

Controlling one's expressions is harder to do than many people realise. Often our faces work independently of our wishes. And usually they communicate our deepest (darkest) feelings, which it may not be in our best interests to reveal. But with a bit of knowledge and practice we can go a long way towards controlling what our faces say.

Becoming aware of the communicative power of facial expressions represents a good start to controlling unwanted communication. Next time you feel that your face may be communicating something that you don't want it to, stop and force yourself to change it. You'll probably find it a little awkward at first, but with a bit of perseverance you should be able to control it at will. With enough practice, it will become second nature.

Smiling

If you were standing outside a room seconds away from being invited in for an interview and I happened to be passing by and you grabbed me with a desperate look in your eye asking me for one piece of advice, I would say, 'Don't forget to smile'.

Smiling is a highly effective communicator and sends all the right signals to the interviewer, especially for building rapport.

A smile can often achieve what the best of answers cannot—softening the interviewer. Very importantly, when you smile at people it usually makes them feel better, which tends to draw out their better nature—exactly what you want to be doing at an interview. It also signals to the interviewer that you have well-developed social skills, are a nice person and do not suffer from anti-social tendencies. Here are some tips about smiling:

- *Be genuine.* Avoid grinning or putting on a forced smile. There's nothing worse than someone trying to smile but only succeeding in demonstrating the art of teeth clenching.
- *Don't overdo it.* Overdoing it may run you the risk of appearing disingenuous.

Avoid mimicking the grim-faced interviewer

It is not uncommon to mimic others' facial expressions (and body language), even though we often don't realise we're doing it. If you encounter the grim-faced interviewer, try not to fall into the trap of being grim-faced yourself. This is not as easy as it may sound because human beings, being what we are, usually require positive feedback in order to continue behaving in certain ways. In other words, if you smile and the other person refuses to smile back, there's a good chance you will stop smiling. So: do not allow a dour interviewer to put you off. Stick to your guns and produce your warmest smiles, no matter what!

Nodding your head

Nodding of the head represents another extremely powerful communicator. When you nod your head at something, people say you are telling them that you agree with them, and you do so without interrupting, which is an ideal rapport-building technique when the interviewer decides to expound on a topic. But be careful: as in smiling, the danger with nodding your head is overdoing it.

Eye contact

The key to successful eye contact is avoiding extremes. Overdoing it can put people off, as can making hardly any eye contact at all. Staring will almost certainly raise a big question mark about your social skills. Even worse, it may frighten the interviewer. Not making enough eye contact will more than likely signal that you lack confidence and perhaps suffer from low self-esteem issues. Bear in mind that interviews are largely about imparting impressions. You may in reality be a confident and outgoing person who enjoys a great social life, but if you fail to make enough eye contact with the interviewer, you will probably fail to communicate that reality.

Like so many of the non-verbal communicators, appropriate levels of eye contact during an interview differ between cultures. It is important that you ascertain the cultural norm before walking into an interview.

Hands and arms

The big mistake with arms is to fold them across your chest. Doing so is tantamount to placing a barrier between you and the interviewer. Other transgressions include sitting on your hands or pretending you don't have any. There's nothing wrong with using your hands to emphasise a point—it shows you're human. However, avoid overdoing it.

Handshake

A good handshake is a firm one. If you are a young male, avoid the primal urge to crush the hand bones of the interviewer. Remind yourself that the purpose of handshaking is to establish rapport, not to demonstrate how strong you are. Avoid also the limp handshake, the long handshake (remember to let go) and the three finger handshake.

If you suffer badly from sweaty palms, bring a handkerchief, but if your sweat glands are running riot it would be a good idea to warn the interviewer first before drenching their palm.

Dress and appearance

Some people persist in thinking that their appearance has very little to do with their ability to perform in a job, and so give little consideration to how they dress for an interview. Whilst the logic in this thinking may be unassailable, it is a dangerous thing to do because it fails to take into account that interviews are largely about *managing perceptions*. Interviewers have certain expectations about dress codes. Failing to meet those expectations is dangerous.

The rule of the thumb for dress and appearance is to err on the side of caution. On the whole, interviewers tend to be cautious and conservative when hiring someone. The last thing an employer wants to do is to hire the wrong person. Reliability, loyalty, consistency, trustworthiness and dependability are qualities that all employers seek in employees, no matter what type of job it is. Your task at the interview is to signal to the interviewer that you have all those qualities, and dressing appropriately represents a good start. Here are some tips:

- Always make a point of wearing clean clothes and shoes.
- Jeans (or anything else) with holes in them may make a positive impression on the dance floor, but are unlikely to inspire an interviewer.
- Avoid excessive jewellery and makeup.
- A designer stubble may make you look manly and represent the latest word from the fashion gurus; however, it's likely to make the interviewer think that you didn't think the job was important enough for you to bother shaving.
- Avoid extreme hairstyles.
- Avoid displaying too much skin.

There is a sensible school of thought that advocates dressing according to the nature of the job you're applying for. So, if you're applying for an accountant's position, you wear a business suit, whereas if you're applying for a labourer's position on a building site, a business suit is inappropriate. All this is true; however, the above tips on dress and appearance remain important.

Interview behaviours

Body language and personal appearance represent one side of the equation to building rapport and trust during an interview. The other, equally important side, is how you behave and express yourself during an interview.

Never argue

One of the worst things you can do at an interview is argue with the interviewer. Even a very polite argument should never be considered. Arguing will more than likely convince the interviewer that you are argumentative by nature, which is not a trait that excites employers. This is a point some interviewees forget—especially when they're convinced they're in the right or the interviewer says something that is evidently wrong. Also, some interviewers (usually inexperienced ones) tend to downplay some of the things interviewees say and add their own information or even make corrections (or what they believe to be corrections). Encountering this type of interviewer can be a very frustrating experience. It is at times such as these that your smile can turn into a grimace and the rest of your body can look like it is ready to launch into battle. However, the effective interviewee will maintain discipline and continue to smile, nod happily and utter little gems like, 'Yes, that's right,' and 'I couldn't agree more'.

You may be thinking, 'I would never want to work for an interviewer who is so disagreeable, so why should I be so agreeable?'

Whilst this is not an unreasonable thought, there are good reasons to ignore it:

- The interviewer may not be the employer or your direct supervisor.
- Bad interviewers do not necessarily make bad employers.
- The interviewer may be inexperienced, nervous or having a bad day.

Always do your very best at an interview, no matter how objectionable you may find the interviewer. The whole idea of attending an interview is to be offered a job. It's up to you on whether you accept the offer or not later on.

Avoid embellishments

It is tempting to exaggerate past achievements—after all, interviews are all about making a good impression. The problem with inflating past achievements is that you can easily lose your all-important credibility, or be caught out later because you've said something different. Embellishments can easily be seen through by experienced interviewers, who will probably not tell you that they think you're gilding the lily, but instead will discount you for the job. This can be a disaster if the interviewer is working for an important employment recruitment firm which handles a large percentage of the jobs you're applying for. It can also be a disaster if you've succeeded in winning the job and fail to live up to the hype you were responsible for starting. It is best to stick to reality.

Avoid negatives

There is no point in attending an interview if you're going to sit there and highlight many of your flaws and defects. Here are some examples of negative statements that send interviewers ducking for cover:

- 'I would have been able to finish the project had I not been clashing with my teammates.' (You may have been working with the teammates from hell, but the interviewer is likely to question your team player abilities.)

- 'I love working in call centres, but sometimes customer inquiries drive me batty.' (A good call centre operator can deal with all types of customer inquiries, including the stupid ones.)
- 'I generally enjoy managing people except when they start complaining about their work. I don't like whingers.' (Most people complain about work from time to time—the job of a good manager is to listen and help, not think of staff as whingers.)
- 'I don't like things changing all the time. Just when you learn one thing you need to unlearn it and learn something different. There's too much instability in some workplaces.' (Unless you're applying for a rare job where things always remain the same, this answer—given today's rapid rate of change—could easily enter the hall of fame for bad answers.)
- 'I don't like pressure.' (Avoid this one unless you're applying for a fantasy job you've created in your head.)
- 'I don't like being told what to do.' (You should be giving serious consideration to starting your own business.)
- 'I suffer from high levels of stress, so I need a stress-free job.' (Another fantasy job.)
- 'I don't like working overtime.' (A lot of people don't like working overtime but it's not the sort of thing to say at an interview. Unless pressing commitments don't allow you to, most jobs require people to stay back sometimes.)
- 'I get annoyed when people don't understand what I'm talking about.' (Perhaps you've got a communication problem.)
- 'I don't know why, but people seem to be frightened of me.' (Perhaps you've got a problem relating to people.)
- 'I'm a slow learner.' (Ouch!)

Negative statements frighten interviewers a great deal—remember, they're a conservative bunch. Being critical about your past performances is tantamount to giving interviewers a reason for not hiring you. Also, negative statements—because they scare interviewers—tend to invite follow-up questions, which is the very last thing you want happening at an interview. The whole idea is to say things that will invite positive questions—that is, questions that allow you to talk about all your strengths and wonderful achievements.

Some people think that pointing out negatives is a way of demonstrating their honesty to the interviewer. Unfortunately for them, the interviewer will only be thinking of ways of terminating the interview. Other than things that will have a direct bearing upon the job (such as a problem back in a job which requires heavy lifting), it is no one's business what your foibles may be. What you may perceive as a weakness about yourself may not be regarded as one by others. At the end of the day, interviews are about making the best impression possible.

Overcoming shortcomings

Not talking about negatives is different to talking about overcoming shortcomings. For many high achievers, work is largely about overcoming shortcomings in their skills and knowledge in order to achieve their aims. Rather than being frightened by new things, they embrace them as learning challenges and look forward to overcoming them. Often the difference between a highly effective employee and one who is struggling has little to do with talent and much to do with this attitude towards learning.

Employers like nothing more than hearing about how you overcame a skills or knowledge deficit in order to complete a project. Overcoming deficiencies demonstrates to the interviewer that you are the sort of person who is able to learn on the job and, as a result, get the job completed. Here's what an 'overcoming a skills/knowledge deficit' answer may sound like:

> After receiving the assignment, we soon realised that some of us on the team did not have the required knowledge to maximise our contribution. My deficit was in understanding how to use several complicated software applications that were crucial to the quality control side of the assignment. My challenge was to learn how to use these applications within a very short space of time and reliably apply this

knowledge. Because we were working under a very tight timeline and the rest of the team were relying on me, there was very little margin for error. Fortunately, I was able to apply my newfound knowledge, as did the other members of the team, and we successfully completed the assignment.

This answer not only tells the employer that you can learn complicated information whilst working on an assignment, but that you can also do it under pressure and deliver the required results.

Dealing with the weakness question: What not to do

The 'What are your weaknesses?' question is not an ideal one for interviewers to be asking. Some of the problems inherent in this question include:

- Many interviewees do not recognise they have a weakness in the first place.
- Others perceive they have a weakness but in fact do not have one at all.
- Some interviewees mistakenly see this question as an opportunity to demonstrate how honest they are and say much more than they should.
- Many interviewees are extremely reluctant to be forthcoming about their weaknesses in an interview.

Despite these problems, many interviewers persist in asking about your weaknesses. Your job is to learn the best way to handle such questions. At the very least, you should be minimising the potential damage and at best you should be turning the question around and demonstrating to the interviewer that you're the sort of person who can not only overcome weaknesses, but by doing so achieve your goals.

One of the worst things you can do in response to answering this question is to say you don't have any weaknesses. This would signal to the interviewer that you had lost some of your grip on reality and/or that you had a monstrous ego, neither of which would do you any favours. Here are some other things to avoid:

- Do not offer more than one weakness and do not set off on a monumental discourse about your failings and their possible origins. Stick to one weakness unless pressed for a second.
- Avoid talking about personality/character type weaknesses such as impatience, quickness to anger or intolerance of mistakes. Generally speaking, these types of weakness frighten employers more than skills deficiencies. Where the latter can normally be rectified with a bit of training, personality/character type weaknesses may be less easy to remedy and more difficult to deal with.
- Avoid clichés such as: 'I work too hard. I don't know when to stop. I don't know how to say no to work requests.' The problem with these answers is twofold: first, a lot of other people use them, which means you're failing to stand out from the pack; and second, all of the above answers may signal to the astute interviewer that you have a serious problem with managing your workload.
- Do not mention things that are really going to hurt you. Mistakes you have made in the dim past should remain in the past. Don't go digging them up—especially if you've learnt the error of your ways and have moved on.

Hopefully, you will not be applying for jobs for which you are unsuited in the first place. If, for example, you have a great fear of heights and part of the job involves working in high locations, then you shouldn't be wasting anybody's time by applying. However, if the same job also requires skills that you have in abundance, feel free to ring first and tell them about your situation. The employer may value those other skills and be willing to at least talk to you.

Warning: If you have committed a legal offence that may be relevant to the job you're applying for, you should investigate what your legal obligations are in terms of disclosure *before* attending the interview. Avoid going on hearsay. Disclosure laws are sometimes changed and may differ from state to state.

Dealing with the weakness question: What to say

An effective way of dealing with the weakness question is to locate the weakness (preferably a skills deficiency) at some time in the past and then describe the steps you took to overcome it (similar to overcoming shortcomings, see above). The idea is that you show the interviewer that you are able to overcome your weaknesses. It's also good to try to finish your answer on a positive note. Here's what an exchange may sound like.

> **Question:** *Tell us about your weaknesses.*
> When I was working for Chaos several years ago, one of my weaknesses was in the area of making presentations to clients and internal staff. Not that my presentations were disasters—far from it—but they lacked the polish of other more experienced presenters. So I approached a presenter whose style I admired and asked her if she could give me some tips on how I could improve my skills. Fortunately, she was very happy to help me, including sitting in one of my presentations and giving me feedback about my weaknesses. I took her feedback on board and made several changes, which led to my presentations improving significantly.

If the interviewer is not happy with this type of answer because it fails to talk about a *current* weakness, simply provide a skills-based weakness that is not going to undermine your chances of winning the job—in other words, a weakness that is not very relevant to the job.

Handling objections

Employer objections usually take the form of 'I like you but . . .' statements. For example, 'I like you, but my main concern is that most of your experience lies in retail which is not relevant to our needs.' You will encounter objections most often when going for promotions or jobs in different vocations or industries. Whilst there is no one correct way to deal with objections (they all need to be dealt with confidently and convincingly), there is a three-step method that you may find useful:

1. Agree with the objection: 'Yes that's correct. Most of my experience does lie in retail.' Agreeing tends to soften the interviewer. Disagreeing will probably make you sound unreasonable, if not desperate.
2. State why you think the objection does not represent a problem: 'I'd like to point out that in retail most of the work I've been doing is directly relevant to this job. Even though the industry is not the same the skills are. For example, the skills required in delivering high levels of customer service and resolving customer complaints are the same as those you require.'
3. Affirm that the difference is not a problem and finish on a positive note: 'In fact I see bringing in a fresh perspective to your business as an advantage. I believe I can introduce new ideas that will drive your business forward.'

Avoid uncertainty

One of the golden rules in interviews is to avoid doubt or hesitancy as much as possible. Saying you can accomplish something with hesitancy in your voice or using tentative language is almost the same as saying that you cannot really do it. Steer away from expressions such as:

- I think I could . . .
- I'm not sure about that but perhaps . . .
- Perhaps I would . . .
- Maybe I could . . .
- I feel that I would be able to . . .

Confidence is one of the keys to establishing rapport in an interview. Interviewers love hearing confident answers because it helps them to overcome their doubt about the interviewee's abilities. Even if you're asked a question about a duty you've never performed before, it is better to say you've never performed it but feel confident about accomplishing it because of all the skills and knowledge you bring to the job, rather than admitting to never having performed the duty and expressing a string of uncertainties. Remember, *how* you say things is more important than *what* you say.

Compare the following answers from two candidates, both of whom are responding to the question 'How do you think you would cope with managing a team of professionals?'

> **Candidate one:** I'm not entirely sure whether I could manage a team of professionals. I've never done it before so it would be a whole new experience for me, but I think with a bit of application I could manage it. Certainly I'd like to have a go. It's an area that I'm very interested in.
>
> **Candidate two:** I'm confident that I could do a good job. I'm comfortable with working with high achievers, I have good interpersonal communication skills and managing people is an area I have a lot of interest in. Even though I've never managed a team before, I feel ready to meet this new challenge in my career.

Essentially, both of the above candidates are saying the same thing. Both are admitting to having no experience in managing a team of professionals, yet both are interested in taking on this new responsibility. The beginning of the first candidate's answer would probably cost them the job, however. I doubt many interviewers would be seriously listening to anything after that first fatal sentence. There is an attempt to recover in the last two sentences but it's too late by then. On the other hand, the second candidate inspires confidence right from the start. There is a complete absence of uncertainty in this answer, even though the candidate admits to having no experience in managing professionals.

Many interviewees struggle with using highly positive language when talking about duties they've never performed before. This is not unusual, given that in non-interview contexts most people use tentative language when talking about things they've never tried before. Your aim should be to leave all tentativeness outside the interview door. If you're not going to be confident about doing a good job, how do you expect the interviewer to be confident about you?

Positive statements

An effective way of getting yourself accustomed to using positive language is to practise using positive statements before the interview. Make a list of positive statements relevant to your situation and start saying them aloud. You may feel a little awkward in the beginning, but repetition will soon take care of that. Keep on practising until you feel very comfortable. Here are some beginnings to help you get started:

- I can definitely do/finish/write/analyse . . .
- I am confident about . . .
- I feel very comfortable at the prospect of . . .
- I am very secure in the knowledge that . . .
- I feel at ease about doing all those things you mentioned . . .
- I am positive about taking on . . .

Start humble and finish humble

The very best interviewees are able to reconcile two seemingly irreconcilable behaviours. They are able to sell themselves at an interview—that is, wax lyrical about all their fine achievements— yet at the same time avoid sounding over-confident or arrogant. The art of remaining humble whilst selling yourself is essential if you are to succeed in interviews because no one likes to work with a person with a bad attitude. Here are some tips on what you can do to get it right.

- *Avoid criticising others.* Even if you had the misfortune of working with the world's most incompetent team it simply does not go down well to be harsh on them in an interview. If you do there's a good chance that the interviewer may think you're trying to big note yourself at the expense of your colleagues. Even if the interviewer is fully aware of how incompetent your colleagues were it still does not pay to be critical. In fact, the opposite is true. The more you avoid criticizing them the more humility will the interviewer see.

- *Third-person statements.* Instead of using first-person statements ('I' statements) all the time, such as 'I did so and so . . .' and 'I am a very good at . . .', it is often better to use third-person statements. The advantage of these types of statements is that they allow you to quote what *others* have said about your achievements, rather than what *you* think. Here are some examples:

  > My boss frequently commented on how quickly I was able to get through my work. (as opposed to 'I was often able to complete my work very quickly')

  > My colleagues, very generously, voted me the most valuable team player.

  > Clients often gave me positive feedback about my customer service skills.

  > The team I worked in consistently gave me top marks for my personal communication skills and willingness to help others.

- *Credit others.* Despite what some people may think, in the vast majority of cases getting something done within the workplace requires the assistance and cooperation of others. Acknowledging the valuable input of others when it comes to your accomplishments is a great way of achieving interview humility. Here's what an answer might sound like:

  > Successfully completing the project on time and within budget meant a great deal to my employer. Had I not delivered the goods, there was the possibility of people being made redundant. However, I would like to stress that the only reason I was successful was because of the valuable help I received from my colleagues. Without their unstinting support I would have failed.

  Without acknowledging the input of colleagues, this answer runs the risk of sounding somewhat arrogant, but the crediting of others ensures that the speaker comes across as humble without reducing the magnitude of the accomplishment.

- *Avoid repeating your key achievements.* In a normal social context, we don't like people going on about their achievements ad nauseum—one mention is generally enough. The same applies in interviews. Whilst it is essential that you learn how to talk up your key achievements, you should only state achievements once. If you repeat them, you risk giving the impression that you either don't have many to talk about or that you're showing off.
- *Avoid 'big noting' yourself.* This may sound a little strange coming from an interview skills book, but it is crucial if you are to avoid portraying yourself as too big for your boots. 'Big noting' yourself means actually saying that you are good or great, or any other descriptor you care to choose—for example, 'I am a fantastic communicator'. It should be left up to the interviewer to infer this by listening to you talk about the sorts of things you've done in this area. In other words, instead of describing yourself, say what you did and how you did it and let those actions speak for themselves. Here are some examples:

Avoid: I was a great manager of people.
Do say: By applying sound principles of people management, I was able to lead my team effectively.
Avoid: I've got great customer service skills.
Do say: My manager often commended me on my customer service skills, in particular my understanding of our products and my ability to link this knowledge to the needs of our customers.
Avoid: I am hard-working.
Do say: In my previous job I always made sure the work was done properly before I went home. If that meant staying back, then that's what I did.

- *Avoid criticising the boss.* We all know that there are mediocre to poor managers out there, and undoubtedly many interviewers have had the misfortune to work for them. Despite this, another of the golden rules is: never criticise your bosses. The reason for this is simple: the interviewer does not have the benefit of listening to both sides of the story and therefore is not in a position to know who was really at fault. In other words, when you criticise your boss, you are effectively creating doubts about yourself in the mind of the interviewer. To criticise more than one boss is virtual interview suicide.

If you're in a situation where the poor performance of your boss prevented you from accomplishing key achievements and you're faced with a persistent interviewer who insists on getting to know the ins and outs of what happened, instead of blurting out something critical about your boss, like 'We didn't achieve our targets because our team leader couldn't tie his shoe laces', you could try something like this:

Unfortunately we came up short of reaching our targets. One of the reasons for this was because certain members of our team lacked the necessary experience to overcome some of the obstacles we encountered. Had we had the right experience, I'm sure we would have succeeded.

Avoid saying anything that may remotely sound like the following:

I had an awful boss.
My boss was a real Nazi.
I couldn't stand my boss and he couldn't stand me.
I wouldn't feed my ex-boss.
My boss suffered from an extremely low IQ.
Nobody liked my boss because he looked like a monkey.

Recruit your voice

Interviewees who know how to use their voices properly enjoy an advantage over those who do not. Your voice is the vehicle by which you deliver your sentences, and you neglect it at your peril. A good interview voice is clear and emphasises important points without too much of a fuss. It is confident and in control, but never overbearing. It rises to the occasion subtly and imperceptibly fades when it has to but always keeps your attention. It is pleasant to listen to.

Here's what not to do:

- Avoid a flat monotone—in fact, avoid any sort of monotone.
- Avoid shouting or raising your voice too high—you'll more than likely frighten the interviewers or have them shouting back at you.
- Avoid an overly soft or shy voice. You don't want the interviewer straining to hear you.
- Avoid extreme changes such as very loud to very soft or very emotional to very measured.

If you've been told, or you suspect, you have a flat or uninspiring voice, practising is the key to changing it. Enlist the help of a good friend or vocal coach.

Building rapport with a panel of interviewers

Everything mentioned so far about building rapport and trust through correct use of body language and the way you say things applies when you are interviewed by a panel of interviewers. Some people feel higher levels of intimidation when confronted by more than one interviewer, but there's no reason for this. The questions are not inherently harder and, if you've done all your preparation, there's a greater chance that your wonderful answers and effective interview techniques will be noticed. There are, however, some simple rules that you need to be aware of before attending a panel interview.

1. *Try to remember everyone's name and use it at least once during the interview.* However, avoid over-use of names because it can sound condescending. If you're one of these people who has difficulty remembering names, or if the panel is a large one, it is a good idea to find out the names of the interviewers before the interview. Simply make a phone call or send an email seeking their names and learn them (it is a lot easier attaching a name to a face if

you already know the name). Remembering the names of all the interviewers on a large panel is impressive and can make an excellent impression. If you happen to suffer a blank and forget a name, stay silent. Do not blurt out a name in the hope that it is the right one! Getting names wrong can spell disaster.

2. *Look at everyone equally.* By looking at someone, you are acknowledging their importance, and by looking at everyone you are signalling strong social skills.

   There are two common mistakes interviewees make when looking at panel members. First, they tend to look only, or mostly, at the person who asks the question. This is a natural tendency but should actively be avoided because it means you are ignoring the others. Second, when interviewees know which member of the panel is highest on the organisational hierarchy, they tend to focus most of their attention on that person. This too can be seen as a natural tendency, but it can be a dangerous approach. Quite apart from the fact that you are effectively belittling the other panel members, you can never be entirely certain who amongst the panel has the real power in making a final decision. It is not uncommon for bosses to defer decisions to one of their staff. By focusing mostly on the boss, you may be ignoring the real decision-maker.

3. *Be very careful not to disregard or pay less attention to panel members who seem not to like you or seem to be ignoring you.* It just might be that one of these panel members is the ultimate decision-maker. In everyday life it would be fairly normal to ignore those who ignore us or who seem not to like us. But in panel interviews you ignore at your peril. If you are confronted by a seemingly difficult panel member, you must try your very best to overcome your natural tendencies and give that person just as much attention as you do the others. To do this you need to be in control of all those subtle negative body language signals that we send out to people we don't warm to (often we do it unknowingly).

   One technique you can employ to help you overcome this problem is to imagine that the fractious panel member is purposely being difficult (playing bad cop) in order to test your interpersonal skills—that is, how you deal with difficult people. If you can see it as a test or a game, then hopefully you can *depersonalise* it and see it as just another challenge that you have to overcome to win the job. And you never know, it might just be a test after all!

Telephone interviews

More and more companies are starting to realise that, because much of their work is done over the telephone, it makes sense to interview candidates using this medium. If you're wanting a job in sales, customer enquiries or any sort of call centre, it would be a good idea to prepare yourself for a telephone interview. Some companies are generous enough to inform you exactly when they will ring you, but many do not. The number one complaint I hear about telephone interviews is that the call invariably comes at a time when people are not ready for it. One minute they're engrossed in a personal conversation, the next they're talking to an interviewer who insists on asking them a range of ugly questions. Given that you cannot put your life on hold for that one telephone call, it makes a lot of sense to prepare a summary of your answers and leave it next to your telephone so that when the call does come, you'll have the main points of your answers right at your fingertips, and can read them out if you have to. This simple strategy is not meant to be a substitute for proper preparation, but it can help you to focus very quickly.

It's all in what you say and how you say it

In terms of content, the answers for a telephone interview should not be any different to the answers you would provide in a normal interview. The fact that a telephone interview does not provide you with the opportunities to 'distract' the interviewer with your dazzling smile and wonderful body language means that there is even more emphasis on what you say. The idea that you do not have to prepare as much because you will not be sitting face to face with the interviewer is a dangerous one.

The big difference with telephone interviews lies in the voice. Whilst voice is important in all interviews, it naturally assumes far more importance in a telephone interview. In fact, one could say that voice is the body language of telephone interviews. Here are some more things to avoid when being interviewed over the telephone:

- long pauses;
- too many 'umms' and 'ahs';
- coughing or sneezing directly over the mouthpiece;
- background noises including television, music, screaming kids, etc.;
- long sighs.

Negotiating a salary

Often interviews contain a discussion about salary expectations. If handled correctly, this can go a long way towards helping you maximise your earnings. Here's what to do.

Give a good interview

It is crucial to understand that salary negotiation starts the second you walk into the interview room, not when the discussion turns to money. In other words, one of the most important things you need to do to maximise what the employer is willing to pay you is to really stand out during the entire course of the interview. Clearly, employers are much more predisposed to giving away more of their money if they think they will be getting value.

Do your research

Trying to negotiate your salary without having done basic research is a bit like trying to hit a target blindfolded. Your research should focus on two areas. First, find out what the market is paying for people such as yourself. You will need to take into account all your qualifications, experience and key achievements. Importantly, you will also need to take into account the industry you will be working in because some industries pay more than others for people of comparable experience and abilities. The same goes with location. Salary survey firms, good recruitment consultants and relevant professional organisations can usually provide you with reliable salary information. Be sure all your sources are credible and that you use more than one. Your case will quickly collapse (as might your credibility) if your sources are found wanting—and they will be if you're facing an experienced negotiator who knows the market. Never go on hearsay and never quote what your friends claim they earn.

Your second area of research should focus on the company itself. You may not be able to get all the information you want, but this should not stop you from trying (just don't make a nuisance of yourself). Things to investigate include:

- *Remuneration policies.* Sometimes, especially with smaller companies, there is a noticeable absence of such policies. However, if they do exist and you're able to access them, you may be able to use this information to your benefit. For example, if you know that the company reviews performance and salaries every six months, you might be able to negotiate a deferment of a higher salary until you've had six months in which to prove yourself on the job rather than accept a lower amount for an indefinite period.
- *Levels of pay.* This can be tricky because information regarding people's pay is often shrouded in mystery. But if you are able to get an insight you will at least know what you're up against. Knowing, for example, that the company is inclined to pay its employees above market value can be a very useful piece of information when negotiating salary.
- *How well the company is travelling.* Companies which are doing well are generally more inclined to pay more than companies which are struggling financially. The last thing you want to be doing is selling yourself short for a company that is riding high.

- *How desperate they are to fill the position.* Some jobs are harder to fill than others, whilst other jobs are crucial to the success of the company. If your research indicates that the position you're applying for happens to fall in either of these categories, then it is reasonable to assume that you have greater leverage in your negotiating.

Avoid mentioning money up front

An important principle in negotiating salary is leaving the discussions right to the end. The idea is to make as good an impression as humanly possible before talk about money arises. This is no different from any salesperson trying to sell a product. Price is only mentioned after all the great features and benefits of the product are discussed. To talk about price before highlighting features and benefits doesn't make for a good sales approach, nor does it make for good salary negotiations. First talk about your skills and knowledge and how they can benefit the business before quoting your price. If you happen to come across an interviewer who wants to talk about money up front, try (politely) to convince them otherwise. You can try saying something like: 'I'd prefer to leave discussion about salary until the end of our talk. I'd really like you to get a better understanding of what I have to offer the company and for me to learn more about the job before money is discussed.' If that doesn't work and the interviewer is adamant, then you're left with no choice—but avoid quoting a specific amount. Instead, quote a range (see below). Doing so will leave you with room with which to manoeuvre later on.

The first principle of quoting employers a range of money that you're willing to consider is realism. Quoting unrealistically high amounts will more than likely damage your credibility and can undo much of the good work you put have in. The following guidelines are designed to help you work out a range.

Establish your bottom line

Give serious thought to determining what *your* bottom line is—that is, the absolute minimum amount you're willing to work for. Three factors you should take into consideration include:

- your cost of living, taking into account expected rises;
- what the market will bear given your levels of experience. Do not go below the bottom point of the market range. If the market range is between $45 000 and $65 000, your bottom line should not go under $45 000. On the other hand, if circumstances are favourable enough, you can exceed the top point;
- how much you want the job. People are often willing to settle for less because of a variety of important personal reasons such as more suitable hours, minimal travelling time or because the job represents the first step to a career change.

Work out a range

Once you've worked out your bottom line, it is important that you stick to it. Accepting a lesser amount will more than likely lead to disappointment later on. Your minimum amount will represent the absolute bottom point of your salary range. How wide you wish to make the range should be contingent upon all the factors discussed above, but mainly on what the market is paying and your levels of experience. Here's one possible approach. Let's say you've decided that your absolute minimum amount is $50 000. You have lots of experience and you know both that the company really likes you and that they have been experiencing difficulties filling the position. You also know that the top end of the market in your industry is $60 000. In such a favourable situation, it would not be unreasonable to quote a salary range starting above your minimum and going above the top end of the market's top end—say, $55 000 to $65 000. If, on the other hand, you know that there is tough competition for the job and your experience is not outstanding, then quoting $50 000 to $58 000 would make more sense.

Another, less conservative, approach to establishing a salary range in the above favourable scenario would be to have the range but quote a higher minimum—say, $60 000 to $65 000. The advantage of this second approach is that it increases the chances of getting the employer to automatically pay your quoted minimum and it fully recognises your powerful bargaining position. A less than flush employer (but one that you're keen on working for) may be frightened off by your expectations, but you should be able to overcome this by agreeing to drop your quoted minimum.

There are no hard and fast rules about establishing either a minimum amount of money you're willing to work for or a salary range. The above guidelines are simply illustrations of possible approaches. The most important thing is to do your research first and then avoid quoting employers unrealistic amounts.

Avoid under-selling yourself

Some people tend to under-sell their services. Experts agree that common reasons for this are a lack of confidence, low self-esteem and the failure of some people to correctly perceive their true worth relative to others. Whilst it is not within the scope of this book to take an in-depth look at overcoming low confidence levels, two important observations need to be made.

One reason a large number of the people I have dealt with undervalue their worth is because they tend to compare themselves with an ideal of perfection rather than with other people. If you are in the habit of measuring yourself against a textbook ideal, you are likely to be setting yourself up for continual disappointment which may be contributing to less-than-ideal confidence levels. The workplace is awash with real people who make mistakes, struggle with motivation, don't have the right answers, are overweight and have wrinkles. Whilst it is a worthwhile pursuit to continually strive for some sort of ideal, it is counter-productive to measure yourself against this ideal when making a value judgment about your worth as an employee.

The second observation regarding people who undervalue themselves is that they often fail to recognise their key achievements and contributions to the workplace. This may be because they've never worked for an employer who gave them their due, or simply because they've never really taken the time to stop and think about their contribution. I am continually amazed at the responses of these people when I ask them what their key achievements have been. More often than not I receive a blank stare, a shrug of the shoulders and the timeless words: 'Not much really. I just do my work.' Yet, after a little prodding and encouragement, a veritable flood of achievements comes gushing forth from the same people. Eyes light up at the realisation that they've been contributing significant things all along but just never saw it that way. An important contributor to this sad state of affairs is that many companies do not measure the outcomes of the work their staff do and thus have no means of passing the relevant information on to them. If you have a haunting feeling that you may be in the habit of under-valuing yourself, it may be time to sit down and have a long hard think about what you've really achieved in the workplace.

If you do your research properly, including what the market is paying for people such as yourself, and you take an honest look at your skills and experience relative to others, you should be able to avoid under-selling yourself. The overriding principle that you should have in the back of your mind is the concept of a fair day's pay for a fair day's work. Anything over that is a bonus; anything under it should be avoided.

Cultural differences

Several years ago, I was talking to a successful recruitment consultant about cultural differences and how they impact on the interview process. Many of this consultant's job candidates came from Asian countries where relationships and expectations between employers and employees are often different from those in the West. One of these differences is in the area of negotiating salary during the course of the interview. In the West, if asked what their salary expectations might be, most people would quote a figure hovering around the mid-range of the current market value of the job. Highly experienced people may seek more, whereas people with less experience would probably ask for a little less in the hope of securing the job. To people familiar with Western negotiating values, this approach makes a lot of sense; however, it is not necessarily how things are done in other countries. In some Asian countries, it is not uncommon for interviewees, when asked what their salary expectations are, to purposely undervalue themselves in order to give the employer the opportunity to offer them more, thus allowing employers to demonstrate their generosity and magnanimity. Failure to comply with this negotiating model could be seen as an act of radicalism or even rudeness, thus cancelling out any chances of being made a job offer. In the West, however, such an approach to salary negotiation could easily lead to the interviewee selling their services well below market value, and thus creating resentment later on. To avoid such problems, the recruitment consultant who first told me about this cultural difference started coaching her job candidates on how to negotiate their salary.

In today's multicultural society, there are many subcultures coexisting side by side. If you happen to belong to one of these subcultures, and are not entirely certain as to the dominant cultural norms of the country you live in, it is important that you make the effort to acquaint yourself with these norms, otherwise you may inadvertently be sending out the wrong signals or selling yourself short. Cultural differences do not just lie with negotiating salary. Potentially they cover a broad range of behaviours, including the things we have covered in this chapter. Sometimes these differences can be subtle, but often these subtleties can make a powerful impression on the interviewer. For example, some non-Western cultures demonstrate their deference to the employer by averting their eyes and not speaking until spoken to. To the culturally unaware Westerner, such outward showing of respect may be interpreted as the behaviour of an overly passive person who lacks confidence.

How to respond when you've been sacked from a previous job

On the whole, employers do not enjoy sacking people. Firing someone is fraught with difficulty and often causes a great deal of angst for both parties. Unfortunately, however, there are employees whose actions give employers no choice but to exercise the ultimate sanction. However, there are also instances in which employees are sacked through no fault of their own. These unfair dismissals can come about from a variety of reasons, including grossly incompetent management, very poor job design (some jobs—especially new ones—have not been thought through and often set people up for failure), poor recruitment practices or lack of training.

The issue here is how someone who has been unfairly dismissed responds to the barrage of questions at their next interview. In particular, how do they respond to the ubiquitous question, 'Why did you leave your previous employer?' when we can reasonably assume that telling an interviewer that you were sacked (albeit unfairly) may border on interview suicide? As already mentioned, interviewers tend to be a cautious bunch (generally with good reason) and have only your word to go by when you try to explain how hard done by you were. Unfortunately, some recruiters (especially in an over-supplied labour market) will demonstrate considerable reluctance to hire someone who was sacked from their last job, even if that person was blameless. Much of their reluctance stems from a fear that the formerly sacked person won't work out in the new job. In such a scenario, the recruiter may end up looking incompetent.

The cold, hard reality is that people who have been sacked from their last job generally start the interview race some distance behind the rest of the field. However, all is not doom and gloom—it just means they have to try that much harder. There are several things such interviewees can do to increase their chances of success.

Describe what happened in detail

One option is to draw a very clear picture of the circumstances that led to your dismissal. One of the keys here is *not* to use pejorative terms. Avoid descending into abusive language or insulting your former employer, hard though it may be. Just stick to the facts and present your case dispassionately, using measured language. Four things you could include to bolster your case are:

- *Similar experiences with other employees.* This is a powerful argument. If others were treated in a similar way to you, then that is compelling evidence condemning the employer.
- *Broken promises.* Employers who dismiss employees unfairly usually make lots of promises which they break.
- *Examples of poor management practices.* These could include any number of things, including: no training where training was essential; significant changes without any warning; zero consultation or feedback; abusive behaviours; or major changes to your job duties without any warning or consultation.
- *What you did to save the situation.* This would include attempts you made to improve matters, including suggestions you made or any actions you took.

Here's what a good answer to the dreaded 'Why did you leave your former employer?' question may sound like:

Unfortunately we parted ways because of a string of negative incidences. My former employer was under some pressure and had great difficulty in coping. He often took out his frustration on his staff, including using abusive language and making all sorts of threats. As a result of this, many of his staff were terrified of him and were actively looking for other work. In fact, staff turnover was very high. He was also in the habit of making important commitments but very rarely keeping them. One example of this was a promise he made that we would receive training on new machinery. This training would have improved our productivity levels significantly and made everyone's life much less complicated, yet the training never arrived. When I approached him about the matter, he told me to mind my own business. When I tried to explain to him that my concern was for the welfare of the business he got very angry and dismissed me on the spot.

Compare the above answer to the following:

I left because I got fired, which was the best thing that could have happened to me. My former boss was terrible. As well as having no idea on how to run a business, he had no people skills whatsoever. He was a bully and an idiot and could not cope with pressure. No one could stand him and those who weren't jumping ship were looking for other work. I got fired because I told him we needed training on new machinery— training he promised we would receive and which would have improved our productivity levels significantly. Last I heard he was going broke, which surprises me not at all.

Even though both of the above answers say essentially the same things, on one level they are complete opposites. The first answer is dispassionate, avoids using abusive language and makes a compelling case before raising the dismissal. By the time the first speaker gets to the dismissal, there's a good chance that he has recruited the sympathy of the interviewer. Whereas the second answer, apart from being abusive and emotional (which would worry any interviewer), begins perilously because it mentions the sacking in its opening sentence. Mentioning the dismissal in your first sentence simply does not give you the opportunity to soften the interviewer.

Avoid mentioning the sacking

The second option involves keeping your mouth shout. Given the stigma attached to sacked employees, it makes little sense to mention the sacking and inevitably frighten the interviewer, especially where your employment period was for a short period of time or performed in the distant past. At the risk of offending those who enjoy occupying the moral high ground, it is my view that there are times when certain things need not be revealed to interviewers. At the end of the day, all employers are entitled to know only whether you can do the job, whether you will fit into the culture of their organisation and what your motivation levels are like.

Group interviews

An increasingly popular form of interviewing is the group interview, in which a collection of interviewees come together and are given a set of tasks to work through as a group (though some tasks may require that you act by yourself, such as giving a presentation).

Examples of group tasks can include any exercise that requires problem-solving, coming up with creative solutions, planning and organising, defining and setting goals or resolving conflict. Whilst the group is working through these tasks, the situation is monitored carefully by an assessor, or a group of assessors, whose job it is to observe how you interact with the group and what your contributions are. Based on your *observable* behaviours—that is, what you say, how you say it, what you do and how you interact with the others in your group—the assessors will draw conclusions about your suitability. In a way, the group interview is the ultimate behavioural interview.

The key to group interviews is to ensure that you *demonstrate the required behaviours* and *avoid undesirable behaviours.*

Desirable and undesirable behaviours at group interviews

Be sure you contribute. Your contribution should be designed to *facilitate the smooth functioning of the group and the completion of the tasks.* Avoid any behaviours that might undermine these two primary objectives. Undermining behaviours can include anything that can reasonably be seen as aggressive or overly dominating behaviour, such as:

- intimidating others;
- insisting on your own way;

- not listening to or dismissing other people's contributions;
- hogging the limelight.

Equally as bad are overly passive behaviours. Sitting there and not contributing, or contributing very little, will do you no favours. It is important that you have the confidence to make a contribution. Don't sit there thinking, 'Oh my God—what if they all laugh at my suggestion?' It is far better to make a less than spectacular contribution than to sit there in silence.

Listen to and acknowledge what other people say. If someone makes a good suggestion, acknowledging it will win you brownie points. But avoid acknowledging for the sake of doing so. And, whatever you do, do not pay homage to every single suggestion.

Where possible, help others—but do it properly. Avoid embarrassing group members or taking over their task.

Don't lose sight of the purpose of the task. If you see the group straying from task, try to bring them back on course by reminding them of the objectives.

Try to work out what behaviours the task has been designed to elicit. For example, if you think the task has been designed to draw out behaviours relating to solving problems within a group, then your job is to demonstrate those behaviours. These might include:

- getting everyone to agree on what the actual problem is (problem definition);
- initiating a discussion on possible causes of the problem;
- finalising the most probable cause/s;
- suggesting a brainstorming session on possible solutions;
- getting agreement on best solutions;
- drawing up a plan of action designed to implement solutions;
- remembering to avoid dominating procedures.

Hopefully I've convinced you of the importance of establishing rapport and trust and that winning a job depends on more than just answering questions correctly. While all of us are different and bring different communication styles to interviews, the experts agree that some behaviours are more effective than others in terms of building rapport and trust. It is important to familiarise yourself with these behaviours so you can maximise your effectiveness.

You may find some of the techniques described above a little difficult to master in the beginning. That's not because they are inherently difficult—in fact, most of them are straightforward. The challenge will be in *unlearning* current behaviours, but with a little perseverance you will be amazed at how quickly you can begin changing; it really is worth the effort to keep at it until you've mastered all the techniques.

Suggested activities

To help you achieve mastery of these techniques, here are some suggested activities to help you along the way.

1. As mentioned above, begin modelling the behaviours of people whose interpersonal skills you admire.
2. Start getting some feedback on how others see you. The challenge here will be getting honest feedback. Because people hesitate to give negative feedback it is worthwhile making the effort to find someone whose opinion you trust and explaining to them the purpose of the exercise. It helps to a) be as specific as possible with the behaviours you want to change and b) monitor your progress. You could monitor your progress by having your helper allocate you a score, say between 1 and 10, every few weeks against each of the behaviours you want to change.
3. You can practice many of the techniques in most social situations. Next time you're having a conversation with someone give some thought to your body language. Does it lend itself to improving communication, rapport and trust? And what can you do to improve it? After a while you'll find that this kind of self-awareness becomes second nature.

Summary of key points

- Building rapport and trust requires three things: answering questions intelligently and honestly; ensuring all your non-verbal communication (body language and personal appearance) does not give cause for apprehension in the interviewer; and conforming to acceptable interview behaviours, such as never arguing.
- Be aware of first and last impressions—people tend to better remember what happens at the beginning and end of any interaction, including interviews. Smiling, using appropriate facial expressions and nodding your head at the right time all give a positive impression.
- For telephone interviews, recruit your voice; it replaces your body language when talking on the phone.
- Remember the key do's and don't's: give credit where it's due and avoid criticising others, including previous bosses; use positive statements but avoid big-noting yourself; mention any shortcomings or hurdles you've overcome but avoid embellishments.
- When negotiating your salary, do your research first—don't undersell yourself, but be realistic in what you ask for. Avoid discussing money before you've highlighted what you can bring to the company.
- In panel interviews, make sure you familiarise yourself with everyone's name. In group interviews, be pro-active in demonstrating behaviours the interviewers are looking for.

10 Effective answers to **common** questions

By now, as well as recognising the basic ingredients of a good interview response, you should also be able to put together your own effective answers. You should know how to:

- find out as much about the job as possible before finalising your answers;
- use the four steps to bring together the major parts of your answers, including what you did, how you did it, the context in which you did it and the outcomes;
- put all your information together so you can articulate clear and coherent answers which do not meander all over the place;
- answer a broad range of questions, including those concerning duties that you have performed before, duties that you have not performed but whose skills you have mastered and duties that you have not performed and don't yet have the skills for;
- use your body language and other interpersonal communication skills to establish and maintain rapport.

There's no simple formula for a good answer

It is important to reiterate at this juncture that, even despite useful guidelines on how to answer questions, there is *no single blueprint or structure for an answer that is applicable to all interview questions.*

Sometimes it may be appropriate to give a three-part answer which includes the context, what you did and how you did it, and an outcome. At other times it may be more appropriate to talk about your ability to do the job, your cultural fit and motivation levels. Often, it may be more appropriate to mix and match from the above. At the end of the day, it is up to you to recognise a suitable structure or approach for each question. And one approach may be just as good as the next—remember, there's no perfect answer. Practice will give you the ability to provide the best possible response.

This chapter presents some good and not so good answers to common interview questions, as well as brief explanations of why they work. By learning to recognise a less effective answer, you should be in a better position to avoid it.

Question: *Why did you choose this job?*
Good answer
Ever since I can remember, I've been interested in this line of work. What attracts me to it is the opportunities it gives me to interact with people, solve problems and work autonomously. I love the fact that one day I could be out on the road helping clients with their problems whereas the next day I can be in my office working with a team of people trying to solve a complex technical problem. I very much enjoy working in a service industry such as ours where I can satisfy clients.

Not so good answer
Actually I stumbled into it quite by accident. I always wanted to be an actor, but getting work was next to impossible. I suppose the reason I'm still in this line of work is because I've picked up all the skills and knowledge and know my way around the traps. I've been doing it for a while now and I suppose you could say I'm an old hand and know how to deliver the goods.

Comments

The first answer responds to the question promptly and then proceeds to highlight the main duties of the job—interacting with people, problem-solving, etc.—as the reasons why the candidate chose the job. Just as importantly, we get a strong sense of the candidate's high motivation levels and the desire to give good service. It also implies that the candidate enjoys working in a team and can do the job, thus addressing the three things employers want to hear.

In the second answer we have to wait until the third sentence before the question is addressed—far too late. Despite the candidate's experience, we get a strong sense of indifference towards the job. We're left with the impression that it's just a job, whereas the first answer is brimming with enthusiasm.

Question: *What factors do you think determine a person's progress in an organisation?*

Good answer

In my view, there are three things that determine a person's progress in an organisation. These are, first, an ability to do the job well, including a willingness to learn new things and adapt to changing circumstances; second, to be able to fit in with the culture of the organisation (i.e. be able to get on with colleagues); and third, to have high levels of drive and motivation. Certainly these are the three things that I insist upon for myself in the workplace. If at any time I feel I'm not at my very best in all three areas, I stop and ask myself what I can do to improve matters. I don't think anyone can truly be happy in their work if all three areas are not being satisfied. So far they've held me in good stead.

Not so good answer

Keeping on the boss's good side is probably the number one thing I can think of. It doesn't matter how good you are—if you don't get on with your boss, I think your days are numbered. Of course, it also helps to be good at your job, but being able to play the game—that is, navigating through the minefield of organisational politics—is I think more important. I realise this may sound somewhat cynical, but all of us know that to get to senior management one needs to know how to play the game.

Comments

A question such as this should immediately be recognised as an opportunity to highlight your strengths. The first answer talks directly about the three things all employers want to hear—ability to do the job, cultural fit and motivation (see Chapter 2)—and then goes a step further and states that all three are qualities that the candidate offers. The second answer is far too cynical and fails to emphasise the candidate's strengths. There is little doubt that an ability to 'play the game' can have a bearing on a person's progress, but to throw all your eggs into that basket is a fatal mistake.

Question: *Why would you like to work for our organisation?*
Good answer
Yours is the sort of company in which I could maximise my contribution. All my research has revealed that you are not only market leaders in service standards and product innovation but that you also have a great work culture. Everyone I've spoken to has talked about the high levels of support, training and recognition employees receive. You offer great career prospects, interesting work and family-friendly policies. Above all, I've always been very keen to work for a company that offers challenging and cutting-edge work.
Not so good answer
I know your organisation really looks after its people—everybody I talked to wants to work here. You pay well and look after your employees. You're a large company, which means that my prospects for career enhancement would be increased and hopefully I wouldn't be doing the same kind of work all the time. I like the idea of getting rotated and learning new things.

Comments

The tone of the first answer is set in the opening sentence, where the candidate talks about wanting to contribute—which is the sort of thing that excites employers. The answer recognises all the good things about the company, but very importantly links these plusses to contribution on the part of the candidate. In other words, it's not just about what the candidate can get from the company but also what the candidate wants to give back.

The overriding problem with the second answer is that it's all about what the candidate can get out of the company. No overt link is made between what the company offers and how these factors can increase the candidate's contribution.

Question: *What do you want to be doing in your career five years from now?*

Good answer

I'd like to be doing what I'm doing now—that is, enjoying my work, working hard and contributing to the best of my abilities. Of course, I'd expect that in five years time my added experience would hold me in good stead for greater responsibilities, which is something I look forward to taking on when the time comes. The most important thing, however, is to be happy, productive and a valued member of the team.

Not so good answer

Basically, I'm ambitious and hard-working, so I expect to further my career considerably. My aim is to work hard and get as far as I can. I think I'd be looking at some sort of management position with greater responsibilities and of course greater rewards.

Comments

There's nothing crushingly wrong with the second answer; in fact, it makes several good points—namely, it gets right to the point and promotes the candidate's hard work and ambition to get ahead. The reason it is not as good as the first answer lies in its limited approach: the candidate's primary goal is one of promotion only. The sub-text is that if there's no opportunity for promotion, the candidate might leave. On the other hand, the first answer acknowledges the importance of hard work and promotion but very wisely goes on to say that getting promoted is not the only thing that matters. The first answer is less egocentric and more aware of the importance of making a contribution to the company.

Question: *Describe your ideal job.*

Good answer

This job that I'm applying for contains many, if not all, of the ingredients of my ideal job. It contains a lot of variety, is intellectually challenging, will allow me to work on my own as well as in a team environment (the best of both worlds), and will also allow me to offer creative solutions to clients. I've always thrived in challenging and results-driven environments and this job offers me all of that.

Not so good answer

My ideal job would be one in which I'd work hard but I wouldn't be too stressed out all the time. It would have lots of variety and a good amount of challenges with plenty of opportunities for advancement. It would include great people to work with as well as a good boss.

Comments

One of the reasons the first answer is so effective is that it links the candidate's ideal job to the actual job in question. Telling an interviewer that the job you're applying for is one you consider ideal makes a lot of sense. Note that all the main ingredients of the job—variety, challenge, working solo as well as in a team environment, and providing creative solutions to clients—would have come under step 1 in the four steps.

Once again, the second answer is not a fatally flawed one. Its major mistake is mentioning stress. The instant you mention stress, the interviewer's alarm bells will start ringing. They'll want to know how much stress is too much and what things stress you out—not what you want to be talking about in an interview.

Question: *What motivates you?*

Good answer

There are lots of things that motivate me in the workplace, but three of my biggest motivators would have to be problem-solving—especially highly technical problems that require specialised knowledge; learning new things and keeping up to date with all the changes in my field; and working in a cooperative team environment where we're throwing ideas off each other and coming up with creative solutions. I love the camaraderie that goes with that.

Not so good answer

Probably my biggest motivator is having a fun job, one I really look forward to and excel in. There's nothing worse than turning up to a job you don't enjoy day in day out. Also, I love having great work hours. I don't mind staying back occasionally and lending a hand, but I wouldn't want to be doing that all the time. I also love working in the city because it's easy to get to from where I live and it gives me easy access to great shops and restaurants.

Comments

The first answer would only be an effective one if the duties mentioned in it—solving highly technical problems, keeping up to date with the latest innovations and enjoying working creatively in a team—were all part of the job description . . . the point is that an excellent strategy for answering the motivation question is to go to the main duties of the job and talk about those (see Chapter 7).

The second answer begins well but fails to mention what constitutes a fun job. Thereafter it is a fatally flawed answer. Working hours and location of work may very well be motivating factors, but they should never be mentioned because they fail to demonstrate how you will add value to the job.

Question: *What qualities do you think are important to be successful in this field?*

Good answer

The qualities necessary to be successful in this field would include the skills and knowledge to actually do the job properly. I'm not just talking about all the technical skills, such as knowing how to operate the various software programs and a comprehensive knowledge of the relevant legislation and how to apply that legislation, but also an ability to get on with people, possess great communication skills and know how to plan and organise your work whilst working under considerable pressure. I also think high levels of motivation and drive are very important. These are all qualities that I possess and can bring to this position from day one.

Not so good answer

The qualities necessary to be successful in this field would include a detailed understanding of all the various software programs required to complete operations. Not only does one require knowledge of how to operate the software but also how to fix things when they go wrong and something is always going wrong. The same can be said for the complex legal technicalities. As you well know, in our industry the devil is in the detail and a superficial understanding of the legislation can lead to a lot of trouble. As well as having a thorough understanding of all the programming requirements of this job, I also have a comprehensive knowledge of the legal subtleties.

Comments

This type of question invites you to go directly to the main duties of the job you're applying for and use those as your answer (it is the same strategy that's used in answering the motivation question). The first answer does just that. It is superior to the second response because it covers more bases. As well as talking about the technical skills, it also talks about getting on with people, planning and organising, and good communication (the generic competencies).

The second answer is not a bad one, but it falls into the common trap of only focusing on the technical side of the job.

Question: *Tell us about a time you handled a difficult situation with a coworker.*

Good answer

Last year one of our colleagues was displaying a lot of aggressive behaviours, including dominating team meetings, belittling other people's ideas and not cooperating. I approached the rest of my colleagues about him and soon realised everyone was feeling the same as I was. We decided not to take the matter to our manager until we had the opportunity to talk to him first. So we decided that at our next meeting we would raise these issues with him. I was chosen to initiate the discussion. At the meeting I avoided personalising the problem and I avoided using inflammatory language. I also adopted an upbeat and optimistic tone. The results were better than we anticipated. He thanked me for the delicate manner in which I raised the issues and also thanked us all for talking to him first before taking it further. After our meeting, his behaviours changed markedly for the better.

Not so good answer

There was one time when one of my colleagues was not pulling his weight, nor was he being at all cooperative with other members of our team. The manager failed to pick it up because some members of the team covered for his mistakes and he would always go out of his way to be extremely friendly when the manager was around. So one day when he was being uncooperative I pulled him aside and let him know what I thought about him. Ever since that day his behaviour towards me changed. He went out of his way to be friendly towards me and he made sure all the work that I needed was done properly. Unfortunately, his behaviour towards the other members of our team did not alter at all. The lesson I learned was that you have to stick up for yourself because no one else will.

Comments

The first answer demonstrates an ability to consult with colleagues, the capacity to solve a problem on your own rather than immediately escalating it to management, and an ability to communicate highly sensitive information in an appropriate manner. It also demonstrates a great outcome for everyone involved. The second answer is too narrow in its focus. It solved the problem only for that individual but fails to address the broader issue of team harmony and cooperation.

> **Question:** *Tell us about a time you had to meet a very tight deadline.*
>
> **Good answer**
>
> When I was working for the Interplanetary Commission, I was required to meet multiple tight deadlines. I was able to consistently meet all my deadlines by adhering to sound planning and organising principles. These included planning my work well ahead so there were no surprises, ensuring that everyone in my team was well trained and well aware of their responsibilities, always having various contingency plans for when things went wrong, and never accepting more work than we could handle. The effectiveness of these practices was highlighted by the fact that my team never missed a deadline and was seen as the standard-bearer for performance within the organisation.
>
> **Not so good answer**
>
> The way I meet tight deadlines is by making sure that I stay back and put in the hard yards. When something unexpected arises or we are experiencing a particularly busy period, I'm not one to shirk my responsibilities. If it means staying back to complete the work on time, I'll do it. In my view there's no substitute for hard work.

Comments

The first answer adheres to the classic components of the four steps. It starts off by providing a context (step 3), then follows up with examples of how deadlines are met (step 2) and finishes by stating positive outcomes (step 4). It gets right to the point, provides multiple examples of how to meet deadlines and states great organisational outcomes. The second answer is commendable because of the candidate's willingness to work hard to get the job done, but it is too one-dimensional. Meeting deadlines requires more than just hard work. It also requires an ability to work smarter.

Question: *What sort of manager would you like to work for?*
Good answer
I'd like to work for a manager who knows how to do his or her job properly as well as knowing how to lead staff. It's important that managers know how to do their job well, otherwise they can lose credibility amongst their staff and a manager without credibility will soon lose the respect that is needed to be an effective leader. My ideal manager would understand and practise sound leadership principles such as consulting with staff, acknowledging people's hard work, providing regular feedback and not intimidating or bullying people. My view is that a good manager is a firm but fair one and knows how to gain the commitment of staff.

Not so good answer
I think it's important for a manager to have good people skills. The best manager I worked for was able to get on with her staff in the workplace as well as outside. She was a good friend to all and everyone knew they could turn to her in time of need. She never turned anyone away and always tried her best to look after us. More people turned up to her farewell dinner than to the general manager's.

Comments
The second answer is too narrow. Good managers need to be more than just liked by their staff. They also need to be good at their jobs and firm with staff when and if the need arises. It's possible that well liked managers may be operating inefficiently in order not to lose popularity amongst staff. The first answer is a more complete

one. Not only does it acknowledge the importance of getting on with people, but it also acknowledges the importance of being firm when the need arises as well as having good work skills.

Question: *Have you performed the best work you are capable of?*
Good answer
Yes I have, and I'd like to think that I do it on an ongoing basis, not just on so-called important occasions. Performing the best work you are capable of, in my view, requires high levels of motivation and a willingness to work hard and learn from your mistakes. These are qualities that I bring to the workplace every day, and I believe the proof of this can be seen in the quality of my work and the praise I have received from former employers. My work on the Odysseus Project, where I exceeded all my targets and played an important role in bringing home the goods, is an example of my daily work rate and contribution.

Not so good answer
Yes I've managed to perform at my best on several occasions. I tend to be at my best when the pressure is on. If I know there's a lot at stake I roll the sleeves up and really give it all that I've got. If that requires working late and on weekends then so be it, as long the job gets done. I love a challenge and enjoy delivering the goods under pressure.

Comments
The strength of the first answer is its argument that performing at one's best is something the candidate does all the time rather than an occasional approach reserved for special circumstances. It also lists the qualities required for someone to perform at their best and then goes on to give a specific example. The second answer is commendable for the candidate's willingness to roll the sleeves up when there's a lot at stake; however, an employer would like that sort of dedication all the time.

Question: *How do you deal with criticism?*

Good answer

I view positive criticism as being the same as constructive feedback—something which is designed to improve my performance, which is important to me. If I'm criticised about an aspect of my work I try my best to locate the source of the problem and do my best to rectify it. Viewed in that light, criticism can be a great learning tool. On the other hand, I do not take kindly to criticism that is not constructive, where the main objective is to hurt or undermine the other person. In such cases I'm inclined to approach my critic in an open manner so we can work things out. I don't think there's a place for negative criticism in the workplace—it just undermines morale.

Not so good answer

I don't like people criticising my work. No one's perfect and I never go around criticising other people's work. Let he who is without fault cast the first stone. Of course, I expect my team leader to criticise my performance if I make a mistake, but I think it's important that the criticism be delivered in the proper manner, with no belittling or bullying. I've seen too many people get crucified over minor mistakes which undermines their commitment to the organisation.

Comments

The first answer's strong suit lies in its ability to distinguish between constructive and negative criticism and its statement of how the candidate would respond to each of those. The second answer's weakness lies in the candidate's reluctance to be criticised by colleagues. Even though the part about belittling and bullying is good, one comes away thinking that the candidate may be a little too sensitive to criticism.

The above answers have been written to give you an insight into what an effective interview might sound like and the reasons employers prefer to hear some answers rather than others. Used in conjunction with the information provided in previous chapters you will be able to construct your own *original* answers that will impress even the most hardened interviewers. Note, however, that while there's nothing wrong with copying key sentences and phrases from the *good answers*, they have not been designed for rote learning. These good answers are meant to provide guidelines for what effective answers might sound like; they're not meant to be entire answers to *your* interview questions. Your own answers will be better because they will stem from your hard-earned experience.

•

Performing well at interviews is not as difficult as many people think. The key to success lies with correct preparation and practice. Knowing what to prepare and how to prepare, then giving yourself the opportunity to apply your newly acquired skills, is a tried and tested formula for success. Remember, great interviewees are not born with effective interview skills—they develop their skills by following this formula.

Completing this book means your awareness of the realities of the interview process has increased significantly. It's also highly likely that your interview skills have already inproved. It is important to note, however, that the more you think about your answers and the more you practice them the better you will become. Great interview skills are not developed overnight; they improve with time and correct application.

Nine key points to remember from this book

1. Don't waste your time looking for quick fixes—they don't exist. They could even make matters worse. Great interview performances come from proper preparation and practice.
2. Avoid memorising other people's answers.
3. Remember that interviews are about more than just giving good answers; they're also about building rapport and trust. And building

rapport and trust is contingent upon more than simply words—body language and attitude are very important.

4. All interviewers want to know three things:
   - whether you can do the job;
   - how motivated or driven you are; and
   - whether you'll fit into the existing workplace culture.

5. Using the four steps gives you a simple-to-follow system by which you can organise and bring together large amounts of disparate information about your work achievements, to help you form clear and articulate answers.

6. The vast majority of jobs have skills or duties that overlap. These include:
   - being a good team player;
   - planning and organising your work effectively;
   - good interpersonal communication skills;
   - ability to cope with change in the workplace; and
   - ability to provide effective customer service (including to internal customers).

   Awareness of these allows you to anticipate the nature of some of the questions you may be asked.

7. Do not fall into despondency if you have a bad interview. Everyone has them, even good interviewees. The key is to learn from it and get yourself ready for the next one.

8. Often, interviewers are not experienced and can ask questions that are not well considered. Your job is to know how to handle both the novice as well as the experienced interviewer.

9. Believe in yourself. Now that you know what to do there's no reason not to.

Good luck.